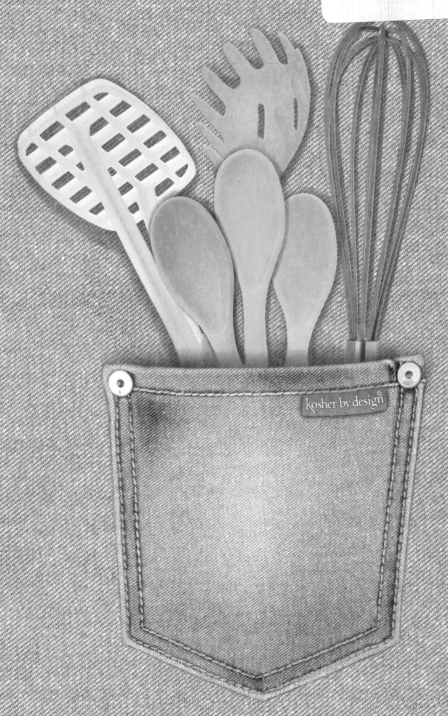

kosher by design

kosher by design
TEENS and 20-SOMETHINGS

cooking for the next generation

By **Susie Fishbein**
best-selling author of the *Kosher by Design Series*®
Photography by John Uher

Published by ARTSCROLL / SHAAR PRESS
4401 Second Avenue / Brooklyn, NY 11232 / (718) 921-9000
www.artscroll.com • www.kosherbydesign.com

Distributed in Israel by SIFRIATI / A. GITLER
6 Hayarkon Street / Bnei Brak 51127 / Israel

Distributed in Europe by LEHMANNS
Unit E, Viking Business Park, Rolling Mill Road
Jarrow, Tyne and Wear, NE32 3DP / England

Distributed in Australia and New Zealand by GOLDS WORLD OF JUDAICA
3-13 William Street / Balaclava, Melbourne 3183, Victoria / Australia

Distributed in South Africa by KOLLEL BOOKSHOP
Shop 8A Norwood Hypermarket / Norwood 2196 / Johannesburg, South Africa

ISBN-10: 1-4226-0998-7 / ISBN-13: 978-1-4226-0998-9

Printed in the USA by Noble Book Press

thank you

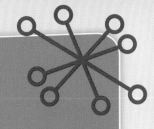

To John Uher and Melanie Dubberly, thank you for making beautiful food. I treasure and appreciate you both for your talents and your friendship. Thanks to their teams: Max Lau, Danny Perretti, Paul Williams, and Lauren LaPenna. These guys can do anything, from catching faces in the food to making a squash wearing sunglasses really rock.

To Renee Erreich of RSEvents, my friend and party planner, and to Elliot Atlas and Atlas Floral Decorators for saying yes before I even had to ask! To Matthew Kolins and Raphi Heimowitz: Larry Sexton left big shoes to fill but you did it with his same "joie de vivre" and style. I know he would have loved this book.

To Gavriel Sanders, thank you for putting words in my mouth, and thoughts in my head, and for being the calm voice on the other end of the line.

To Damian Sansonetti and Lito Tan for always putting on a show in my kitchen.

To Dr. Stuart Ditchek, Dr. Lori Zucker, and Debbie Minsky for your special diet/allergy input.

To Tzini Fruchthandler, I think by now you can almost read my mind. Thanks for always being one step ahead of me.

To Eli Kroen, Elizabeth Parsons, Felice Eisner, Judi Dick, Elisa Greenbaum, and Karen Finkelstein; thanks for your eagle-eyed precision.

To Aviva Whiteman, who took this book to the finish line with spunk and flair. Thank you for paying attention to every last detail, you made my work so much better.

To Gladys Estrada, *muchas gracias* for being helpful and calm even when things got crazy and messy.

To the ArtScroll/Mesorah family and Gedaliah Zlotowitz, happy 10th anniversary to us. What a wonderful experience it has been. And of course, gratitude to Hashem for all of the above and for all of my blessings.

dedication

This book is dedicated to:

ATARA BLUMENTHAL, RINA FUCHS, SHARI MANN, ESTEE STEIN; four girlfriends who saw me through my teens, twenties, and beyond.

And to my parents LINDA AND LENNY SPECTOR who survived it all with a smile.

And to my favorite teens, tween, and adorable little fella KATE, DANIELLE, JODI, and ELI — you make every day a joy.

Most importantly, I dedicate this book to my amazing husband KALMAN — can you believe we have teenagers?

INTRODUCTION

Got the study munchies?

Friends coming over to hang out?

Helping your family with dinner?

First time living on your own?

Many young kids help out in the kitchen with a batch of cookies or brownies. Once you are old enough to be responsible for your own food, there are so many reasons to find your way into the kitchen other than for a sweet dessert. Cooking is a skill that will serve you well. It is easy to go the "pizza or takeout" route, but that can be unhealthy, uninspired, and expensive. Explore new ingredients; discover that cooking can be quick, easy, and rewarding. Good food is also a great excuse for gathering friends and family.

If you can read, you can cook. Making a recipe is nothing more than reading and following directions step-by-step. More importantly, once you get into it and learn how flavors meld and how ingredients behave, you will develop your own personal style, freeing yourself from this or any cookbook. So turn up some music, grab a skillet and spatula, and let's get cooking!

Tastebuds

Thanks to the following teens and 20-somethings for coming over to share a meal and an honest opinion. I hope you enjoy this book, the fruits of your labor.

Zach Blank	Hana Fusman	Alex Mendelsohn	Daniel Sheris
Alex Botwinick	Jenny Grad	Simon Mendelsohn	Alex Stadtmauer
Lia Botwinick	Taylor Heller	Shoshana Oster	Julianna Stadtmauer
Eric Brauner	Rachaili Hubsher	Samantha Plotsker	Matt Stadtmauer
Michael Chapman	Zellie Hubsher	Dina Raab	Emily Stone
Aaron Dardik	Avigayil Jarashow	Alec Rabinowitz	Eitan Sufian
Alex Eagle	Leeora Judas	Danielle Rabinowitz	Nathan Ullman
Pneena Feldman	Leora Kagedan	Rachel Roth	Emily Weiss
Danielle Fishbein	Aviva Kahn	Ariana Schanzer	Kevin Wolf
Eli Fishbein	Nina Kahn	Orah Schlanger	Dalya Zucker
Jodi Fishbein	Jordan Klahr	Adina Schwartz	Rachel Zucker
Kate Fishbein	Rachel Kor	Eli Schwartz	Nicole Zweiter
Alex Fuchs	Erica Langer	Yosefa Sebrow	
Deena Fuchs	Hannah Lebovics	Noah Shechter	
Lauren Fuchs	Eytan Mendelow	Reuven Shechter	
Lilly Rose Fuchs			

Table of Contents

stuff we like

getting started

Nothing is quite as rewarding as sitting down to a meal you have made yourself. Make the most of your time in the kitchen. Write down your menu and shopping list and see what ingredients you already have on hand. Right from the start, plan on making enough for leftovers or select other recipes that use some of the same ingredients. Cooking for friends or family? Check for allergies and vegetarian/vegan needs.

▷ Preparation

Always read through a recipe before getting started, to make sure you have all the ingredients and enough time to prepare the dish. Take the time to pre-measure your ingredients so you can cook like a pro. Have each item chopped, peeled, scooped, cut, measured, and waiting to be tossed into the pan. I like using paper-lined muffin tins to keep ingredients organized. This also allows for a quick cleanup instead of washing multiple bowls or ramekins. Sort through the recipes and work out timings for oven use. Arrange your racks before turning on your oven to preheat.

▷ Setting up

Keep a kitchen timer handy or use the one on your oven or microwave — it's easy to get distracted and forget when something went into the oven, especially if you're making more than one recipe at a time.

Do a body check. Roll up your sleeves, secure loose clothing, tie your hair back, make sure you are wearing non-slip shoes that also protect your feet from hot drips. Wet a kitchen towel and wring it out. Use it to anchor your cutting board to your counter so it doesn't slide around when you are cutting. Keep an oven mitt or small kitchen towel handy for holding the handles of a skillet or pot — they heat up when on the fire.

Wash your hands with soap or glove up with disposable gloves and you are ready to cook!

▷ Cleaning up

At the back end of cooking comes cleaning. Make sure you clean as you go so you are not left with a counter full of dirty pots and pans at the end. The longer you let dirty stuff sit, the harder they are to clean. If a dish is simmering or baking, use that time to put ingredients away, wipe down countertops, wash and dry pots, etc. Use hot soapy water to clean; it is more effective than cold water in breaking down oils. Make sure all ovens and stovetops are turned off. Your parents, roommates, suitemates, or spouse will beg you to cook if it also means that you have left your space clean.

healthy eating... tips

Nutrition experts agree: A healthy body should get a variety of at least five fruits and vegetables per day for more optimal health. Fruits and veggies are great sources of vitamins, minerals, antioxidants, and phytochemicals (aptly pronounced "fight-o-chemicals"). These are substances that naturally occur in plants, and many of them may yield health benefits beyond anything your body can absorb from a multivitamin.

It's important to eat fruits and vegetables of many different colors, since each color group carries unique nutrients. If you eat at least one cup from each color group, you're on your way to getting your five servings per day. So go ahead and eat the rainbow!

*Shop this cookbook
and plan your menus:

Cooking your own food is the surest and healthiest way to develop good eating habits. Fast food may be convenient and tasty, but even with healthier menu choices, fast foods still contain high salt and fat content. By making your own food, you control portion size and ingredients.

Plan your meals carefully. There is room in a healthy diet for all foods, just not all at once. If you eat a less-healthy choice for lunch, balance your diet with a healthier dinner.

Coming home starving to an empty fridge usually leads to unhealthy choices and grabbing whatever's around. If you plan your menus in advance, you can make sure you have ingredients on hand. You can balance the types of foods you need in a day and make sure you are ready to cook them.

Eating a variety of foods throughout the day plays a big role in leading to a healthier diet.

At **breakfast**, try throwing berries into a bowl of whole-grain cereal.

Combine frozen and/or fresh fruit with some yogurt in a blender and start your day with a nourishing smoothie.

For **lunch,** add additional chopped or cut-up veggies to a salad or to a scoop of tuna or egg salad for a more filling meal.

Pack a small bag of nuts and seeds to carry you through a midday munchie craving.

Start **dinner** with a vegetable-based soup; it will fill you up and help get some of the vital servings of veggies into your diet.

Portion size is the key. Try to follow the half-plate guide: Divide your plate in half. Fill one side with veggies, fruit, or salad and the other half with your protein, grains, and a side dish.

Equipment

You don't need a lot of fancy stuff to get going in the kitchen. Here is a list of all the equipment used in this book.

BASICS: mixing bowls ✳ skillet ✳ jelly roll pans ✳ cookie sheets ✳ oven-to table baking pans ✳ metal baking pans ✳ tube pan ✳ microplane

TOOLS: can opener ✳ silicone spatula ✳ wooden spoon ✳ pastry brush ✳ rolling pin ✳ metal spatula ✳ whisk ✳ knife ✳ cutting boards ✳ tongs ✳ potato masher — optional ✳ parchment paper ✳ strainer ✳ ladle ✳ measuring spoons ✳ measuring cups, liquid and dry ✳ cupcake tin ✳ garlic press

SAFETY: disposable gloves ✳ oven mitts ✳ fire extinguisher

BIG-TICKET ITEMS: immersion blender ✳ food processor ✳ blender — optional ✳ stand mixer

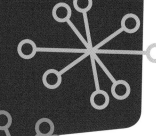

special diet needs

Anyone with food sensitivities will appreciate these convenient sidebar symbols that indicate vegetarian, gluten-free, dairy-free, and nut-free recipes.

Follow the signs:

(V) **Vegetarian:** A vegetarian is a person who refrains from consuming meat, poultry, and fish. The broadest definition of a vegetarian, a lacto-ovo vegetarian, may include dairy products and eggs. The strictest form of vegetarianism is vegan, defined as one who eats plant foods only and avoids all animal by-products. A pescatarian abstains from eating all meat and poultry but does include fish. A pescatarian is not technically a vegetarian, but some people adopt this kind of diet for health reasons, as fish is high in Omega-3 fatty acids. In this book, a recipe marked with a (V) represents lacto-ovo vegetarians, so if you don't eat eggs or dairy products, avoid or adapt those recipes as well.

(GF) **Gluten-Free:** Gluten is the basic protein component of grains such as barley, rye, wheat, and spelt. This means gluten is found in most types of cereals and in many types of bread. Not all foods from the grain family, however, contain gluten. Examples of grains that do not have gluten include rice, wild rice, corn, buckwheat, millet, amaranth, quinoa, and teff. Certain grains, such as oats, can be contaminated with wheat during the growing and processing stages of production. It's not clear whether oats harm most gluten-free dieters, but doctors generally recommend avoiding oats unless they are specifically labeled gluten-free.

Some people suffer from celiac disease, a condition which impedes the digestion of gluten. As a preventive measure, individuals with celiac disease must eat foods that do not contain gluten protein. In addition, care must be taken when purchasing store-bought packaged foods and ingredients.

Gluten is often not apparent in store-bought products such as some salad dressings, beverages, Worcestershire sauce, mayonnaise, corn tortillas, and others. So, if a recipe is marked with a (GF), make sure to buy and use the gluten-free version. For example, regular soy sauce contains wheat, but wheat-free soy sauce, known as Tamari, is easy to find. Recipes using soy sauce thus are marked gluten-free. Ingredients like pasta, teriyaki, hoisin sauce, and others are available gluten-free but may be harder to find. Recipes using these ingredients are not noted as gluten-free, but if you can find the gluten-free kind, you can convert those recipes as well. So, if you are gluten-free, make sure that you are using versions of the ingredients that are wheat-free. There are even breads that are available gluten-free. Read labels carefully. Natural health markets as well as a growing number of conventional stores are stocking many gluten-free options.

Dairy-Free:
A dairy-free diet contains absolutely no dairy products; no milk, butter, cheese, cream, whey, casein, or yogurt. People who follow a dairy-free diet may include lactose-intolerant individuals, individuals with irritable bowel syndrome, or vegans.

A lactose-free diet means eating foods that have no lactose, a sugar that is a normal part of milk products. Some people do not break down lactose well. They may not have enough lactase, the enzyme that breaks down lactose in the body. Some people have a partial lactase deficiency, which allows them to eat only a minimal amount of dairy before developing symptoms or discomfort. Lactose intolerance can develop at any age and may only be transient as it can occur after gastrointestinal infections. Others may produce lactase that does not work properly, leading to gastrointestinal problems.

In this book, dairy-free recipes are marked with a (DF). Many recipes can be made dairy or parve, so when cooking for someone on a dairy-free diet, make sure you use the parve version of a recipe. Work with milk substitutes such as soy milk, rice milk, nut milks, and milk-free products, including soy cheese, soy cream cheese, soy sour cream, and margarine. Store-bought prepared foods are totally dairy-free when marked *kosher parve*.

Nut-Free:
Nut allergies have become increasingly common. Peanuts aren't actually a true nut; they're a legume (in the same family as peas and lentils). But the proteins in peanuts are similar in structure to those in tree nuts. For this reason, people who are allergic to peanuts may also be allergic to tree nuts, such as almonds, Brazil nuts, cashews, chestnuts, filberts, walnuts, hazelnuts, macadamias, pistachios, pine nuts, and pecans. A recipe in this book that is marked with an (NF) is nut-free. Make sure that you purchase less obvious foods in their nut-free forms; for example, pretzels can be bought nut-free. Read packages on prepared items. Some factories clean their machines between runs of food production that contain nuts. Not all cleaning processes eliminate the dust that may remain from nut-containing manufacturing. Highly allergic individuals should buy their most reliable brands that they have used over time. If a reaction occurs in a product labeled nut-free, they should be very careful to avoid that product in the future. Seeds are not nuts and allergic people often use them in cooking as substitutes for tree nuts. However, be aware, sesame is a potent and common allergen, so check with your nut-allergic eaters to see if they are allergic to sesame as well. Take note, recipes in this book that contain sesame are still marked (NF).

a few notes about ingredients

lways use unsalted butter in sticks. Salt is added to butter to preserve freshness. Use unsalted for the cleanest, freshest flavor. This way you can control the amount of salt added to your recipes.

Unless otherwise stated, these recipes use size large eggs. Eggs do vary in volume and recipes can be affected if you use jumbo or other sizes.

Measure liquids in liquid measuring cups and dry ingredients in dry measuring cups. The volume of wet and dry ingredients differs, requiring separate measuring cups for accuracy. Using a liquid measure for dry ingredients and vice versa may alter the outcome of a recipe, especially in baking, where ingredients mix in a precise chemical way.

For better taste and texture, I use fine sea salt, coarse sea salt, or kosher salt, rather than table salt. The recipes specify which kind to use.

Low-fat versions of cheeses, milk, or sour cream may be substituted, except where specified. Sometimes the higher-fat version is needed for taste, texture, or meltability.

In recipes that call for chocolate, always use good-quality bars that you would enjoy eating. Chocolate chips were designed to hold their shape, so they are not ideal for melting. Make sure you use good-quality chips as well, made from real chocolate, not just chocolate flavoring.

When selecting nonstick cooking spray, I use high heat or professional, made by companies like Pam®. These sprays retain heat longer without burning, and tend to stain your cookware less.

>> Safe food habits:

- Thoroughly wash your hands with soap and water before and after handling foods.
- Wash all fruits and veggies.
- Wear disposable gloves when handling raw meat, poultry, or fish. Keep their juices away from other foods.
- Cook poultry and meat until they are done. Poultry should not be pink when cut into. Use a meat thermometer when in doubt. Ground meats should be cooked to 160°F minimum and poultry to 165°F.
- Wash the tops of cans before opening.

- Thaw frozen foods in the refrigerator or microwave, not for long periods on the counter.
- Don't leave raw or cooked food out for too long at room temperature or bacteria will grow.
- Buy a thermometer for your refrigerator and make sure the temperature stays at or under 40°F to keep food safe. A freezer should be set at zero degrees or below.
- Freeze cooked leftovers or use them within four days.
- Have a fire extinguisher handy in case of flare-ups and be sure you are familiar with how to use it.

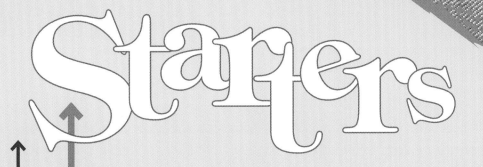

Starters

Cranberry Chicken Dippers

MEAT ■ YIELDS 6 SERVINGS

wooden skewers

3 boneless, skinless chicken breast halves

1 (14-ounce) can whole berry cranberry sauce, divided

1 tablespoon chili sauce

1 tablespoon hot sauce, such as Tabasco® or Frank's® RedHot®

2 cloves fresh garlic, minced

2 tablespoons dark or light brown sugar

2 tablespoons soy sauce

½ teaspoon ground ginger

2 tablespoons canola oil

People love food on a stick and this dish is no exception. The cranberry dipping sauce adds a shot of bright color and flavor. It also goes well with turkey, so make some extra sauce and bake on turkey parts.

1. Soak the wooden skewers in a pan of water for at least 10 minutes.

2. Place the cutlets, one at a time, into a heavy-duty ziplock bag or between 2 sheets of parchment paper. Using a meat pounder or bottom of a skillet, pound each cutlet until it is ½-inch thick. Repeat with remaining cutlets. Slice the chicken cutlets lengthwise into ¾-inch wide strips; place in medium bowl.

3. In a microwave-safe bowl, place ¼ cup cranberry sauce, chili sauce, and hot sauce. Heat in microwave for 30 seconds on high; remove and stir until smooth. Pour over the chicken strips and toss to coat well.

4. Allow the chicken to marinate while you prepare the dipping sauce. Pour the remaining cranberry sauce into a small pot. Add the garlic, brown sugar, soy sauce, and ginger. Heat over medium, whisking until the mixture is smooth and slightly bubbling. Turn off the heat.

5. Folding the chicken strips slightly, weave them onto the skewers, accordian-style.

6. Heat the oil in a large skillet, griddle, or grill pan, or brush it on a preheated outdoor grill. Add the skewered chicken strips and sear for 2–4 minutes per side until cooked through and no longer pink. Do not crowd the pan; you may need to do this in batches.

7. Transfer to a platter. Pour the dipping sauce into a ramekin, small bowl, or on the plate, and serve the chicken with the dipping sauce.

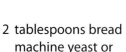

Hot Pretzel Challah

PARVE ■ YIELDS 2 CHALLAHS

2 tablespoons bread machine yeast or active dry yeast

1 tablespoon sugar

½ cup lukewarm water

3 tablespoons sugar

2 cups water

1½ teaspoons fine sea salt

¼ cup canola oil

6 cups bread flour (King Arthur® brand if possible)

8 cups water at room temperature

⅔ cup baking soda

pretzel salt, kosher salt, or sesame seeds

mustard, optional for dipping

The ballpark meets the Shabbos table! Unlike most challah recipes, this one can't be frozen because the challah will get soggy when it is defrosted and reheated. In fact, it is best made fresh or at most one day ahead, but cool completely before putting in a plastic bag and rewarm before serving. You can order pretzel salt from the internet or save the packets from boxes of store-bought frozen hot pretzels. A selection of mustards, such as spicy brown, coarse grain, and honey-mustard, will make this a home run.

1. In a medium glass or Pyrex bowl or measuring cup, place the yeast, 1 tablespoon sugar, and ½ cup lukewarm water. Proof the yeast: it should show signs of life by expanding, slightly bubbling, or moving. If none of these things happened, your yeast is dead. Spill it out and start again.

2. Meanwhile, in the bowl of a stand mixer fitted with a dough hook, on medium-low speed, mix the 3 tablespoons sugar, 2 cups water, fine sea salt, and oil. This can also be done by hand with a whisk.

3. When the yeast has been "proofed" and shows signs that it is alive, beat the yeast mixture into the mixing bowl. With the mixer at a low speed, add the flour. Raise speed to medium and knead for 4–5 minutes until a nice, smooth, satiny dough forms. It will have almost a matte finish. If you are kneading in the flour by hand, it may take a few minutes longer to get a good smooth texture. Cover the bowl of dough with a kitchen towel and allow the dough to rise in a warm place for 1½ hours or until doubled in size.

4. Preheat oven to 350°F. Line a jelly roll pan with parchment paper. Set aside.

5. Remove the dough to a lightly floured surface. If the dough is sticky, knead in flour, a little bit at a time, until the dough is easy to roll. Divide the dough in half. Divide each half into 3 balls and roll each into a long strand. Braid each challah using 3 strands of dough. Place on prepared cookie sheet. Set aside to rise while you prepare the next step.

6. Bring the 8 cups water and baking soda to a boil in a pot with the widest opening. Gently and carefully, lower one challah into the baking

soda solution. Using 2 wooden spoons, carefully turn the challah so both sides get a good exposure to the water or bathe the top of the challah with spoonfuls of the solution. After 30 seconds remove the challah to the parchment-lined pan, using the 2 spoons to support it. Repeat with the second challah.

7. Once both challahs are back on the pan, brush with the water from the pot and sprinkle with salt or sesame seeds.

8. Bake for 30 minutes. Best served warm or rewarmed. Serve with mustard.

Big Dogs in Blankets

MEAT OR PARVE ■ YIELDS 8 SERVINGS

high heat or professional cooking spray

8 reduced-fat hot dogs, turkey dogs, chicken dogs, or soy dogs

1 small can (8-ounces) vegetarian baked beans

½ cup sauerkraut, drained

mustard

relish

1 box (2 sheets) frozen puff pastry, at room temperature for 30 minutes to defrost

1 egg

2 tablespoons water

The most popular pass-around at simchas — in a mega-size! This dish, a dog stuffed with the works, can be made using reduced-fat beef, turkey, chicken, or soy hot dogs.

1. Preheat oven to 475°F.

2. Line a jelly roll pan with parchment paper. Spray the parchment with cooking spray and set aside.

3. Using the tip of a knife, cut a slit along the length of each hot dog, using your fingers to spread the hot dog open a little.

4. Using a 1-teaspoon measure, spoon 2 teaspoons of the baked beans into the slit along the length of each hot dog. Spread 1 tablespoon sauerkraut over the beans on each dog. Drizzle each with mustard and relish.

5. Open the puff pastry sheets. Cut each puff pastry sheet into 4 long rectangles (against the folds if using Pepperidge Farm Puff Pastry®). Place one hot dog toward the bottom of a pastry strip. Spiral the pastry strip around the filled hot dog. Pinch at the top to secure the end of the pastry strip. Place on the parchment paper.

6. Repeat with remaining hot dogs and pastry.

7. In a small cup, using a fork, whisk the egg and water. Brush the pastry with this egg wash.

8. Bake for 7 minutes. Rotate the pan to bake evenly and bake for an additional 7 minutes. Place on platter or plates. Serve hot.

Fiery Goodness™

Jamaican Jerk Chicken Wings

MEAT ■ YIELDS 6 SERVINGS

NF

DF

GF

18 chicken wings, cleaned of feathers

3 scallions, roots trimmed and discarded, cut into 3 pieces

1 small onion, peeled, quartered

2 jalapeño peppers, with seeds, stems trimmed, halved lengthwise

3 cloves fresh garlic

¼ cup soy sauce

¼ cup red wine vinegar

¼ cup olive oil

2 tablespoons dark brown sugar

2 tablespoons lime juice, fresh or bottled

1 tablespoon fresh thyme leaves

½ teaspoon ground cloves

½ teaspoon ground allspice

¼ teaspoon ground nutmeg

Jerk seasoning is native to Jamaica. It is a hot spice rub that adds great flavor to meat, chicken, or fish. If you want a crazy-hot spice level, use a Scotch Bonnet pepper instead of the jalapeño. Either way, remember to wear disposable gloves when handling hot peppers and don't touch your eyes, nose, or mouth.

1. Preheat oven to 400°F.

2. Line a jelly roll pan with aluminum foil. Place the chicken wings in a single layer on the prepared pan. Set aside.

3. Place the scallions, onion, jalapeños with their seeds, garlic, soy sauce, vinegar, olive oil, brown sugar, lime juice, thyme, cloves, allspice, and nutmeg into the bowl of a food processor fitted with a metal "S" blade. Process until smooth. Transfer to a bowl.

4. Brush both sides of each wing with some of the marinade. Place wings skin side down on the prepared pan. Bake for 35 minutes.

5. Remove the pan from the oven. Set the oven to broil. While the oven is heating, use tongs to turn over each wing. Brush the wings again with the remaining marinade. Return to the oven and broil for 4–5 minutes until chicken is done. Remove the wings to a plate or platter and top with the pan juices.

Turkey Sliders

MEAT ■ YIELDS 16 SLIDERS

1 pound ground turkey, a blend of white and dark meat if possible

¼ cup teriyaki sauce

½ teaspoon dried thyme

½ teaspoon garlic powder

¼ teaspoon freshly ground black pepper

⅛ teaspoon dried sage

2 tablespoons olive oil

slider buns or hamburger buns

2 plum tomatoes, each cut into 8 slices

½ cup plus 2 tablespoons favorite barbecue sauce

½ cup nondairy sour cream

toothpicks

Here's something quick, good, and good for you too! The small size of these sliders makes them irresistible. Ground turkey is lean, which makes it a healthy choice, but it can tend toward the dry side. When experimenting on your own with ground turkey, make sure you add some kind of moisture, the way this recipe uses teriyaki sauce in the mix.

1. Place the ground turkey into a large mixing bowl. Pour in the teriyaki sauce. Sprinkle in the thyme, garlic powder, black pepper, and sage. Using your hands, mix to distribute the spices.

2. Heat the olive oil over medium heat in a large nonstick skillet. Scoop 1 tablespoon of the turkey. Using wet hands, form a patty about the width of the slider buns. Repeat with remaining turkey. You should get 16 patties. Place into the hot pan; do not crowd. Cook for 1½ minutes per side. Do this in batches if they don't all fit.

3. If you can't find mini slider buns, make your own using a small round cookie cutter and hamburger buns. Dip the cookie cutter into warm water. Cut 2 mini buns from each hamburger bun.

4. Place a slider on each bun. Top with a tomato slice, a dollop of barbecue sauce, and a dab of parve sour cream. Cover with the top of the bun. Use a toothpick to secure.

5. Transfer to serving platter or plates.

dainty and delicious

Mexican Pizza Empanadas

1 tablespoon canola oil

¾ pound lean ground beef

3 tablespoons taco seasoning (from a 1.25-ounce packet)

1 small onion, peeled and cut into ¼-inch dice

1 plum tomato, cut into ¼-inch dice, with seeds

½ cup jarred salsa, mild or medium

1½ pounds pizza dough, or frozen pizza dough, defrosted

all-purpose flour, for dusting

1½ tablespoons nondairy sour cream, such as Tofutti® Sour Supreme, divided

extra-virgin olive oil

bottled taco sauce

These were the crowd favorite at their testing. You can find parve frozen pizza dough balls in many supermarkets. Defrost according to the package directions.

1. Preheat oven to 375°F. Line a cookie sheet with parchment paper. Set aside.

2. In a medium skillet, heat the canola oil over medium heat. Add the beef and cook the meat until it is no longer pink, breaking up the chunks with a wooden spoon or the tip of a silicone spatula. Add the taco seasoning and sauté for 3–4 minutes.

3. Transfer the meat to a medium bowl. Add the onion, tomato, and salsa. Mix well.

4. Using your fingertips, flatten the dough. Divide into 8 equal pieces.

5. Dust your work surface with flour. Using a rolling pin, roll out each piece into an oval shape. Place ¼-cup meat filling toward the bottom of the oval but leave room at the edge. Top the meat with ½ teaspoon parve sour cream. With a wet finger or pastry brush, moisten the bottom edge of the dough. Bring the top half over the bottom, enclosing the meat.

6. Using the tines of a fork dipped in flour, press down all around the edges to seal the empanada. Place on prepared sheet. Repeat with remaining dough, meat, and non-dairy sour cream.

7. Bake for 20 minutes. Brush with olive oil for sheen. Serve with taco sauce.

Camp Lavi Fricassee

MEAT ■ YIELDS 10 SERVINGS

1 pound lean ground beef

½ small onion, peeled and cut into ¼-inch pieces

1 slice white bread

1 large egg

2 tablespoons canola oil

1 medium onion, peeled and cut into ½-inch pieces

1½ pounds chicken necks

¼ cup all-purpose flour

2 cups water

3 tablespoons canola oil

2 pounds (about 20) chicken wings

1 cup chicken gizzards, optional

1 tablespoon paprika

1 tablespoon dry onion soup mix

2 teaspoons chicken consommé powder

4 cups (32-ounce box) chicken stock or broth

Fricassee is one of the foods that link us all to our summer camp memories. In the summertime, I have been lucky enough to go to Camp Lavi to teach cooking to the teens. One summer, I got the beloved Chef Alex Daich to tell me the secrets of his famous fricassee. At that time, he had worked at camp for 13 years, as well as serving for 25 years as the cook for Stern College. His instructions were for a batch to feed 400, so I had to tinker at home to make it a more manageable amount. I tested it on past Lavi campers and they loved it — I hope you will too.

1. In a medium bowl, mix the ground beef and ½ small onion that was cut into ¼-inch pieces. Wet the slice of bread and squeeze out the water. Tear the bread into tiny pieces and add it to the beef along with the egg. Using your hands, mix well to combine. Roll into small meatballs. Set aside.

2. Heat 2 tablespoons canola oil in a very large (14-inch) skillet or pot. Add the onion and sauté for 4–5 minutes, over medium heat, until golden and translucent. Do not allow the onion to burn; If it starts to brown, lower the heat.

3. Add the chicken necks. When their meat turns white (about 3 minutes), use tongs to turn each neck. Cook for another 2 minutes. Sprinkle the flour over them.

4. Add the water and simmer for 20 minutes over low heat. Stir with a wooden spoon every few minutes.

5. In a separate skillet, heat the 3 tablespoons canola oil. Add the meatballs, shaking the pan to rotate them so that they brown on all sides.

6. Add the browned meatballs, chicken wings, and gizzards, if using, to the pot. Sprinkle in the paprika, onion soup mix, consommé powder, and chicken stock or broth. Cook, uncovered, for 30 minutes at a low simmer.

7. Ladle into bowls and serve hot.

Mexicali Squares

DAIRY ■ YIELDS 12 SERVINGS

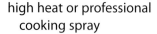

high heat or professional cooking spray

2 tablespoons chili powder

1 tablespoon dried oregano leaves

2 teaspoons ground cumin

1 teaspoon garlic powder

½ teaspoon onion powder

1 teaspoon coarse sea salt or kosher salt

½ teaspoon freshly ground black pepper

2 tablespoons canola oil

1 (12-ounce) box Smart Ground® Original Veggie Protein Crumbles

1 large yellow onion, peeled, cut into ¼-inch dice

3 large plum tomatoes, cut into ½-inch dice

1 (15.5 ounce) can black beans, drained and rinsed

1 cup creamed style corn

4 large eggs

2 cups milk

1 cup pancake and baking mix, such as Bisquick®

2 heaping cups (8-ounce bag) grated cheese, either cheddar or Pepper Jack

½ cup finely chopped cilantro

¾ cup low-fat or fat-free sour cream or non-fat plain yogurt

3 cups finely shredded lettuce

jarred salsa, heat level as desired (optional)

Mexicali, the capital city of Baja California, Mexico, is the inspiration for this "half-Mexi"–"half-Cali" dish. This vegetarian appetizer is filling enough to be served as a main dish. Just add a fresh green salad like the Tex-Mex on page 80 and you have a hearty, healthy meal. My food stylist and friend Melanie Dubberley gave me this recipe. It is a version of a dish her mom used to make for her when she was a kid.

1. Preheat oven to 375°F. Spray a 9-by-13-inch baking dish liberally with cooking spray. Set aside.

2. In a small bowl, combine the chili powder, oregano, cumin, garlic powder, onion powder, salt, and black pepper. Set aside.

3. In a large sauté pan, over medium high heat, heat the oil and sear Crumbles until crispy, about 6–7 minutes. Add the spice mix. Cook 1 minute longer; add the onion and tomatoes, and cook another 2 minutes. Add the black beans and corn and heat through. Dollop the cooked mixture into the baking dish, and use a spatula to gently spread it to the corners.

4. In a medium bowl, add the eggs and milk to the pancake mix. Whisk thoroughly. Pour over the Crumbles. Gently poke down into the Crumbles with the spatula so the liquid sinks to the bottom evenly.

5. Bake for 25 minutes. Carefully remove the pan from the oven and sprinkle with grated cheese. Bake for an additional 10 minutes, until cheese is melted and just starts to brown.

6. Meanwhile, in a small bowl, stir the cilantro into the sour cream and set aside.

7. Remove the casserole from the oven and let cool 10 minutes.

8. Cut into 12 squares and place them on a platter or individual plates. Top each with about ¼ cup of shredded lettuce and about one tablespoon of cilantro sour cream. Drizzle salsa over each if desired.

Stuffed Mushrooms

DAIRY OR PARVE ■ YIELDS 20 STUFFED MUSHROOMS

20 crimini or baby bella mushrooms, brushed clean

2 tablespoons olive oil

½ onion, peeled, finely chopped

2 cloves fresh garlic, minced

½ teaspoon dried thyme

½ teaspoon fine sea salt

½ teaspoon freshly ground black pepper

½ cup panko breadcrumbs

6 fresh basil leaves, finely chopped

6 fresh chives, finely chopped

¼ cup cream cheese or nondairy cream cheese

If your chopping skills need some sharpening, you can just toss the mushroom stems, onion, garlic, and spices into a food processor fitted with a metal "S" blade. A few pulses, and you're ready to continue with the recipe.

1. Preheat oven to 400°F.

2. Use a dampened paper towel to brush off any dirt from the mushrooms. Remove mushroom stems and set them aside. Place the mushrooms stem side up on a foil-lined jelly roll pan.

3. Finely chop the mushroom stems.

4. Heat the oil in large pan over medium heat. Add the mushroom stems, onion, garlic, thyme, salt, and pepper. Sauté for 4–5 minutes, until fragrant and the mushrooms start to release some of their liquid.

5. Sprinkle in the panko breadcrumbs and mix well. Cook for 1 minute more.

6. Remove from heat and stir in the basil, chives, and cream cheese. Mix well. Stuff into the mushroom caps, making rounded mounds.

7. Bake for 25 minutes. The mushrooms will soften and the stuffing will be golden brown.

Munchies

so good!

Chocolate Fluffernutter Quesadillas

DAIRY ■ YIELDS 4 QUESADILLAS

4 large flour tortillas

8 tablespoons reduced fat creamy peanut butter

8 tablespoons Marshmallow Fluff®

1 (4-ounce) good-quality milk chocolate bar, such as Ghiradelli®

high heat or professional cooking spray

Peanut butter with marshmallow fluff sandwiches are a popular shalosh seudot meal at my house. This version is instant gooey gratification and a great filling snack or meal.

1. Place the tortillas on the work surface in front of you.

2. Spread the bottom half of each tortilla with 2 tablespoons peanut butter.

3. Spread 2 tablespoons marshmallow fluff over the peanut butter.

4. Break one ounce of the chocolate bar and arrange the pieces over the fluff.

5. Bring the top half of the tortilla over the bottom to cover the filling.

6. Preheat a large nonstick skillet over medium heat. Spray with nonstick cooking spray.

7. Place 1–2 quesadillas into the pan. Cook for 1 minute, flip each, and cook for 1 minute on the other side. Remove. Repeat with remaining quesadillas.

8. Cut into wedges and serve immediately.

Frozen Banana Pops

DAIRY OR PARVE ■ YIELDS 9 FROZEN BANANA POPS

popsicle sticks

3 ripe, firm bananas, no brown spots

1 cup peanuts, lightly salted, chopped in food processor, or other topping of choice

2 cups best quality semi-sweet or milk chocolate chips

1 tablespoon canola oil

You will need craft sticks or popsicle sticks for this recipe in order to make the bananas easy to dip and look like lollipops. Thin skewers will not be able to support the weight, so if you don't have the popsicle sticks, you can cut the bananas into slices and make bite-size pieces. They will still be yummy.

Although I usually melt chocolate in the microwave, for this recipe use a double-boiler to keep the chocolate warm and smooth throughout the dipping process. Partially freezing the banana first helps; the chocolate will coat thinly and dry quickly.

There are so many toppings that you can try: graham cracker crumbs, Rice Krispies®, crushed cookies, granola, sprinkles, shredded coconut, toffee bits, crushed almonds — the choices are endless. Hey, why not throw a frozen banana party and let your friends decide how to top theirs! To get the pops to stand up, like in the picture, cover a piece of styrofoam or floral oasis with tissue paper or wrapping paper. Stick the pops right in for a fun centerpiece.

1. Line a plate or flat aluminum tin with parchment paper.

2. On another plate or tin, spread the nuts or other topping of choice. Set aside.

3. Peel the bananas and cut each into 3 pieces. Insert a popsicle stick into each piece of banana. Place on parchment-lined plate and freeze for 20 minutes.

4. Meanwhile, heat the chocolate chips and canola oil in a heat-proof bowl set over a pot of simmering water. This creates a double boiler. It keeps the chocolate off the harsh direct heat and allows it to melt slowly and smoothly. Make sure the water does not bubble into the bowl or the chocolate won't melt properly. Stir the chocolate well. When it is melted and smooth, remove the bananas from the freezer.

5. Holding one banana pop by the stick, use a small metal offset spatula or dull knife to cover the bananas with chocolate in a thin even layer. Hold the banana on an angle to allow excess chocolate to drip back into the pot.

6. Immediately roll banana in the chopped nuts or other topping, so all surfaces are coated.

7. Repeat with remaining bananas. Once all the bananas are coated, pour any leftover nuts onto the parchment-lined plate and rest the bananas on them in a single layer. Return them to the freezer for at least 15 minutes or up to a week.

8. If bananas are completely frozen, allow them to stand at room temperature for 10–15 minutes before eating.

Raspberry Iced Tea

PARVE ■ YIELDS 8 SERVINGS

3 raspberry flavored
  tea bags
3 black tea bags,
  such as Lipton®
3 cups cold water, divided
½ cup sugar
  ice cubes
1 cup clear apple juice
lemon, optional
mint sprigs, optional

It has probably been years since your lemonade/iced tea stand days. The little cuties on my block are out there often but they are hawking drinks straight from the mix. Homemade iced tea doesn't contain any kind of additive and the taste is incomparable. Refresh yourself and whip up a tall cool glass of this tea. Always start with fresh, cold water and experiment with various kinds of tea bags. As an alternate flavor, substitute 3 orange spice tea bags for the raspberry flavored ones and add the zest of a small navel orange while the tea bags are steeping. Garnish with slices of the zested orange.

1. Carefully remove any paper attached to the strings of the tea bags; tie the strings together.

2. In a medium pot, bring 2 cups cold water and the sugar to a rapid boil. Remove from heat. Wait until the bubbles subside. Add the tea bags and steep for 10 minutes. Don't let them steep longer or the tea may turn bitter. Remove tea bags and discard.

3. Fill a large (about 2-quart) pitcher with ice cubes. Add 1 cup cold water and the apple juice. Slowly pour the tea into the pitcher. If using a glass pitcher, don't pour too quickly or the hot tea may crack the pitcher; pour tea slowly over the ice so that it can cool down.

4. Add a squeeze of lemon and sprig of mint if desired.

Veggie Corn Fritters

DAIRY OR PARVE ■ YIELDS 10 FRITTERS

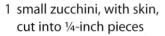

1 small zucchini, with skin,
  cut into ¼-inch pieces

1 cup broccoli florets

1 cup cauliflower florets

water as needed

1 large egg

1 cup milk or plain
  unsweetened soy milk

1 tablespoon canola oil

½ teaspoon fine sea salt

2 cups dry cornbread mix

2 tablespoons all-purpose
  flour

canola oil for frying

jarred marinara sauce,
  warmed, for dipping

This recipe has a parve option, but some of the cornbread/muffin mixes are dairy, so shop carefully. Also, they vary in size, so you may need 2 packs; just make sure you have at least 10 ounces of mix before you begin the recipe.

1. Place the zucchini into a 2-cup measuring cup. Break the broccoli and cauliflower florets into tiny florets, cutting away the thicker stem parts.

2. Add enough of the tiny broccoli and cauliflower florets to the zucchini to make 2 cups. Place into a microwave-safe bowl. Cover with water. Microwave on high for 4 minutes, until the vegetables are soft. Drain and set aside.

3. In a medium bowl, whisk the egg, milk, tablespoon canola oil, and salt. With a silicone spatula, stir in the cornbread mix and stir until a smooth batter forms.

4. Sprinkle the flour over the drained cooked vegetables. This will keep them from sinking to the bottom. Mix vegetables into the batter, using your spatula to distribute them evenly.

5. Heat ½-inch canola oil in a large skillet over medium heat. You will know the oil is ready when you drop a tiny amount of batter into the pan and it sizzles. If it sizzles too vigorously, turn the heat down. Use a ¼-cup measuring cup to add the batter to the pan; do not crowd. Depending on the size of your skillet, work with 3–4 fritters at a time. Use a metal spatula to flatten each fritter as the batter hits the pan. Fry for 2–3 minutes per side, until golden brown. When flipping the fritters, flip away from your body to prevent splattering yourself with hot oil.

6. Drain on paper towels. Serve with warm marinara sauce.

Mexican Hot Chocolate

DAIRY ■ YIELDS 4 SERVINGS

CINNAMON STICK GARNISH:

- 4 large cinnamon sticks
- 1 (4-ounce) good-quality semisweet, white, or milk chocolate bar (I like Ghiradelli®), chopped

HOT CHOCOLATE:

- 1 (4-ounce) good-quality semisweet chocolate bar
- 4 cups milk
- 2 tablespoons sugar
- 1 teaspoon ground cinnamon
- ½ teaspoon pure vanilla extract
- ⅛ teaspoon almond extract

A few years back I led a culinary tour in Israel. At the end of the trip, one of the participants, Nadine Ben-Baruch, sent me a goody bag of Israeli gourmet specialty items, including stunning chocolate-dipped cinnamon sticks. The mix of cinnamon and chocolate got me thinking about Mexican hot chocolate. Some Mexican hot chocolate recipes contain chilies and other spices. I kept this one sweet with only the addition of cinnamon but included the stunning garnish. Swirl it around your mug to infuse your steaming drink with melted chocolate and perfume from the stick.

1. Prepare the cinnamon sticks: Line a paper plate with parchment or wax paper. Place the chopped chocolate into a small microwave-safe bowl. Microwave at 70% power for 30 seconds at a time, stirring for a full 10 seconds at each interval to hasten the melting, until smooth and melted. Dip the bottom half of each cinnamon stick into the chocolate. Place onto the prepared plate to set.

2. Place the second chocolate bar onto a cutting board. Using a large knife, thinly slice it so that it breaks into small shavings. Set aside.

3. Pour the milk into a large pot. Add the sugar, cinnamon, and chocolate, including all the tiny shavings that are on the cutting board. Bring to a simmer over medium-low heat. Whisk to make sure the chocolate is melted and the milk is hot, about 8 minutes.

4. Remove from heat. Stir in the vanilla and almond extracts.

5. Ladle into mugs. Serve each with a chocolate-dipped cinnamon stick for stirring.

Spicy Garlic Bread

DAIRY OR PARVE ■ **YIELDS 8-10 SERVINGS**

1 (22-by-2-inch
  or 15-by-3-inch) French
  or Italian bread

½ cup (1 stick) butter or
  margarine

2 cloves fresh garlic,
  minced

½ teaspoon garlic powder

1 teaspoon dried oregano
  leaves

½ teaspoon dried basil

½ teaspoon crushed red
  pepper flakes

¼ teaspoon fine sea salt

A great accompaniment to salad, soup, or a bowl of pasta.

1. Preheat oven to 375°F. Line a cookie sheet with parchment paper. Set aside.

2. Place the bread on a cutting board. Using a serrated knife, make cuts every inch, but do not cut the bread through to the bottom; leave the slices attached at the base. Place on a rectangle of foil that is large enough to fully wrap the loaf.

3. Melt the butter or margarine in a microwave-safe bowl. It should take about 45–50 seconds.

4. Stir in the minced garlic, garlic powder, oregano, basil, red pepper flakes, and salt.

5. Using a pastry brush, brush the butter-garlic mixture over the top and between the slices, making sure to brush the inside of the slices so that all exposed surfaces are coated.

6. Bring edges of the foil together to enclose the loaf and place on prepared cookie sheet. Bake for 15 minutes, until heated through.

7. Serve immediately.

Refreshing!

Apple-Walnut Greek Yogurt Dip

DAIRY ■ YIELDS 4 SERVINGS

Ⓥ
ⒼⒻ

1 cup low-fat 2% Greek yogurt

high heat or professional cooking spray

¼ cup honey

¼ teaspoon ground cinnamon

2 large Honeycrisp, Granny Smith, or other apple

½ cup chopped walnuts

A quick, healthy snack for between meals or anytime. Greek yogurt is thick and creamy and a little more tart than regular yogurt. It also wins out in the protein and probiotic categories when compared to regular yogurt.

1. Measure the yogurt into a small mixing bowl.

2. Spray a ¼-cup measure with nonstick cooking spray. This will help the honey slide right out when measured. Add the honey and cinnamon to the yogurt. Mix well.

3. Slice the apples into rings or wedges, discarding the core and seeds. Arrange on a plate. Drizzle with yogurt dip.

4. Sprinkle with walnuts. Serve cold.

Pink-Berry Lemonade

PARVE ■ YIELDS 6 SERVINGS

3 cups watermelon (flesh from 1-2 pounds seedless watermelon)

10 medium strawberries, hulled

4 cups water

¾ cup sugar

1 cup lemon juice, fresh or bottled

½ cup unsweetened cranberry juice

For a fun garnish on your glasses or pitcher, trim off any pink flesh from the watermelon rind, leaving ½-inch-thick rind. Place the rind on a cutting board, green side down. Place a star-shaped cookie cutter over the rind, hold a wooden spoon over the cookie cutter and press with all your weight to cut out and form the star shape. Make a slit in the corner of the star and fit it onto the rim of the pitcher or glass.

1. Place watermelon and strawberries into the bowl of a food processor fitted with a metal "S" blade. Pulse until the fruit is puréed.

2. Heat the water and sugar in a large pot over medium heat. Stir until the sugar is completely dissolved. Remove from heat.

3. Place a strainer over the pot. Pour the puréed fruit into the strainer. With a wooden spoon, press down on the fruit to release all the juices into the pot. Discard the remaining solids.

4. Add the lemon juice and cranberry juice to the pot. Mix well. Transfer to a pitcher. Chill until cold.

5. Serve over ice cubes.

thirst-quenching!

Spicy Barbecue Popcorn

PARVE ■ YIELDS ABOUT 8 CUPS

½ cup popcorn kernels

3 tablespoons canola oil

1 tablespoon barbecue spice mix (I like Chef Paul Prudhomme's Barbecue Magic Seasoning®)

1 teaspoon smoked paprika

This is the version my family loves, and the hotter the spice, the better! You can cut the heat by cutting down on the amount of spicing. Try other popcorn variations, such as mixing the hot popcorn with the powdered cheese packet from a box of Wacky Mac® for a dairy cheddar cheese popcorn.

1. Pop the popcorn in an air-popper. If you don't have one, place the kernels and oil into a large pot with a tight-fitting lid. Put on oven mitts. Turn the heat to medium. Holding the lid and the pot at the same time, cook the popcorn over medium heat, shaking the pot the entire time. Popping should start in about 2–3 minutes; continue shaking the pot. Make sure the kernels are moving around so they don't burn. Once the popping slows, remove the pot from the heat but wait a few more seconds for the kernals to finish popping before you remove the lid.

2. Empty the popcorn into a very large bowl. While the popcorn is still hot, toss on the barbecue spice and smoked paprika and stir to distribute the spices.

Scones

DAIRY ■ YIELDS 20-24 SCONES

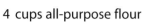

4 cups all-purpose flour

½ cup sugar

2 tablespoons baking powder

1 teaspoon fine sea salt

11 tablespoons (1 stick plus 3 tablespoons) butter, at room temperature for 15 minutes

2 eggs, plus one additional for brushing

½ cup milk

6 tablespoons mix-ins such as chocolate chips, blueberries, or raisins, optional

Eighteen years ago, when my niece Lauren was born, she had a baby nurse named Eileen. When Baby Lauren would wake to eat in the middle of the night, so would Nurse Eileen. She would shuffle into the kitchen and whip up batches of these delicious scones, leaving some for us family visitors. A gorgeous new baby in the family plus delicious fresh scones made their apartment a popular hangout for our whole family.

1. Preheat oven to 375°F.

2. Line 2 cookie sheets with parchment paper. Set aside.

3. In a large bowl, whisk the flour, sugar, baking powder, and salt.

4. Cut the butter into small cubes. Add it to the flour mixture and use both hands to knead the dough, rubbing the butter into the flour.

5. Add the eggs and milk, kneading to form a crumbly but somewhat sticky dough.

6. Turn the dough out onto your work surface and knead for another minute or two; the dough should start to become more smooth as the butter softens from the warmth of your hands. Divide the dough into two pieces. Use the heel of your palm to spread each piece into a circle, about ¾-1 inch thick.

7. If adding any mix-ins, spread them over the dough, then knead and press into a circle. Do not over-mix the scones.

8. Using the mouth of a drinking glass or a round 2-inch diameter cookie cutter, cut out circles of the dough and place 2 inches apart on the prepared cookie sheets. Re-roll the scraps, and cut out more scones.

9. With a fork, whisk the remaining egg. Using a pastry brush, brush generously over the tops of the scones.

10. Bake for 15 minutes or until bottoms are golden brown and tops are light golden. Remove from oven and place on cooling rack.

11. Serve warm or at room temperature.

Trail Mix

1 cup dry roasted peanuts

1 cup whole unsalted almonds

½ cup raw cashew halves

½ cup good-quality chocolate chips

½ cup sweetened dried cranberries

½ cup dried blueberries

½ cup chocolate-covered raisins or yogurt-covered raisins

½ cup raw shelled sunflower seeds

Whether you are hiking over to your couch to study or hiking a long trail, trail mix is a quick and easy, high-energy snack that will satisfy your munchie hunger. The dried fruits and chocolate will satisfy your sweet tooth. If you are taking trail mix with you for a hike or picnic, keep in mind that the chocolate may melt, so you may want to skip the chips and the yogurt/ chocolate-covered raisins. Create your own stylized mix with other dried fruits, dried berries, coconut, banana chips, granola, or cereal.

1. Combine all the ingredients in a large bowl. Stir to distribute evenly. Store in an airtight container.

Soups and Salads

Tomato Eggdrop Soup

MEAT OR PARVE ■ YIELDS 4 SERVINGS

Eggdrop soup, with its wispy strands of egg, is a popular item on Chinese take-out menus. It couldn't be easier to make, so try it at home. Feel free to add cubes of chicken or tofu for a whole meal in a bowl.

1 beefsteak tomato

1 teaspoon toasted sesame oil

¼ teaspoon ground dried ginger

4 cups chicken or vegetable stock or broth, divided

2 teaspoons cornstarch

pinch of ground white pepper

½ teaspoon soy sauce

2 large eggs, plus 1 yolk, lightly beaten

2 scallions, roots trimmed and discarded, thinly sliced on the diagonal, for garnish

1. Cut the tomato through its belly. Squeeze and scoop out the seeds. Discard the seeds. Cut the tomato into 1-inch pieces.

2. Heat the sesame oil in a soup pot over medium heat. Add the tomato and sprinkle with ginger. Cook for 2 minutes, stirring the whole time. Add 3¼ cups stock or broth and bring to a simmer. Allow to simmer for 1 minute.

3. In a medium bowl whisk the cornstarch with the remaining ¾ cup stock until smooth. Slowly pour it into the pot while whisking.

4. Add the white pepper and soy sauce. Simmer for 3 minutes.

5. While swirling the soup in one direction with the whisk, pour in the eggs in a steady stream, continuing to stir in the same direction.

6. Ladle into bowls and garnish with chopped scallions.

Orange Butternut Squash Soup

MEAT, DAIRY, OR PARVE ■ YIELDS 6 SERVINGS

1 tablespoon olive oil

1 medium onion, peeled, cut into ½-inch dice

20 ounces frozen butternut squash cubes

1 cup baby carrots

1 Honeycrisp or Braeburn apple, peeled, cut into cubes, seeds and stem discarded

¼ teaspoon ground ginger

⅛ teaspoon ground nutmeg

⅛ teaspoon chili powder

½ cup juice from tangerines or clementines (about 4-5), or store-bought orange juice

4 cups (32-ounce box) chicken or vegetable stock or broth

½ cup heavy cream or plain unsweetened soy milk

If you mind the little bit of pulp that the clementines or tangerines add, strain before adding to the soup, or use store-bought orange juice instead.

1. Heat the olive oil in a large soup pot over medium heat.

2. Add the onion and sauté for 3–4 minutes until translucent; do not allow to brown.

3. Add the butternut squash, carrots, and apple. Stir.

4. Sprinkle in the ginger, nutmeg, and chili powder. Stir.

5. Pour in the juice and stock. Allow to simmer on low heat, uncovered, for 20 minutes or until a fork can easily pierce the squash and carrots.

6. Transfer the soup in batches to a blender or use an immersion blender right in the pot; purée the soup until very smooth.

7. Stir in the cream or soy milk.

8. Ladle into mugs or bowls.

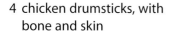

Chicken Noodle Soup

MEAT ■ YIELDS 8 SERVINGS

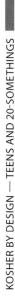

4 chicken drumsticks, with bone and skin

4 chicken thighs, with bone and skin

water as needed

1 onion, peeled

1 turnip, peeled

2 large carrots, peeled

2 large parsnips, peeled

2 stalks celery

2½ teaspoons coarse sea salt or kosher salt

small bunch fresh dill, bottom stems removed

small bunch fresh parsley, bottom stems removed

8 ounces dried Kluski or other shaped egg noodles

If you are making the soup in advance, don't add the noodles until you are ready to serve.

A slotted soup skimmer is an inexpensive utensil that works well in this recipe.

1. Place all the chicken pieces into a large soup pot. Add enough water to come up 3 inches over the chicken. Bring to a boil over medium heat. As the foam rises to the top, scoop it out and discard.

2. Add the onion, turnip, carrots, parsnips, celery, and salt.

3. With one of the parsley sprigs or with a piece of kitchen twine, tie the parsley and dill together. Lower into the pot. Cover. Reduce heat and simmer for 1½ hours. Turn off the heat.

4. Scoop out and discard the onion, turnip, celery, and parsley/dill. Remove the carrots and parsnips. Slice them and return them to the pot.

5. Using tongs, remove the chicken parts and place them on a cutting board. Discard the skin. Using 2 forks, shred the chicken meat and return it to the pot, discarding the bones.

6. Add the noodles to the soup and return to a simmer. Cook 10-15 minutes, until the noodles are al dente.

7. Ladle into bowls and serve hot.

Beef and Barley Soup

1 cup pearled barley

4 cups (32-ounce box) chicken stock or broth, divided

2 tablespoons olive oil

2 pounds flanken (3–4 strips)

3 large or 5 small shallots, peeled and sliced

3 large cloves fresh garlic, sliced

1 teaspoon sugar

8 ounces sliced button or crimini mushrooms

2 teaspoons Dijon mustard

¼ teaspoon dried thyme

2 tablespoons margarine

2 tablespoons all-purpose flour

4 cups (32-ounce box) beef stock or broth

½ cup cooking sherry

Comfort food at its best. As soon as they smell this soup cooking, you'll find everyone comes running for a good, filling winter warm-up.

1. Place the barley into a medium pot. Add 3 cups chicken stock or broth. Bring to a boil. Turn down to a simmer and cook, uncovered, for 20–25 minutes, stirring occasionally to make sure it is not burning or sticking, especially toward the end of the cooking time. The barley is done when the grains are plump and all broth is absorbed. Remove from heat.

2. Meanwhile, in a large pot, heat the olive oil over medium heat. Add the flanken. Sear for 3–4 minutes until brown. Using tongs, turn each strip over and sear the other side until brown. Remove from the pot; set aside.

3. Place the shallots into the pot and use a wooden spoon to help scrape up all the good browned bits that the beef left behind. Cook until the shallots are shiny, about 3 minutes. Add the garlic and sugar. Stir well and cook for 3 minutes longer, until the garlic is fragrant.

4. Add the mushrooms and Dijon mustard. Crumble in the dried thyme. Stir. Cook the mushrooms for 4 minutes, until shiny and beginning to release their liquid.

5. Add the margarine and melt it into the mushrooms. Stir.

6. Sprinkle the flour over the mushrooms. Mix until the mushrooms and shallots become sticky and look dry.

7. Pour in the beef stock or broth, the cooking sherry, and the remaining cup of chicken stock or broth. Stir. Bring to a simmer.

8. Once the stock or broth is simmering, cut the flanken between each bone. Return the meat to the pot. Cover and turn the heat down to a simmer. Cook for 30 minutes.

9. Spoon a portion of barley into each bowl. Ladle the soup over the barley.

Pizza Soup

DAIRY ■ YIELDS 6 SERVINGS

1 French or Italian bread

½ cup olive oil, divided

1 large or 2 small onions, peeled, cut into ¼-inch pieces

5 cloves fresh garlic, thinly sliced

1 tablespoon dried oregano leaves

2 (28-ounce) cans whole peeled tomatoes

½ cup water

1½ teaspoons fine sea salt

¼ teaspoon freshly ground black pepper

2 cups fat-free skim milk

4 ounces shredded mozzarella cheese

Why order in? This recipe has all the makings of pizza … in a bowl!!! Your friends will flip when they dig into the cheesy baguette and you will love how easy it is to make.

1. Preheat oven to 375°F. Line a jelly roll pan with parchment paper. Set aside.

2. Cut 6 (1-inch-thick) slices from the bread.

3. Measure ¼ cup olive oil into a small dish or bowl. Lightly dip both sides of each bread slice into the oil. Place on prepared pan and toast in the oven for 8–10 minutes, until golden. Remove the bread and preheat the broiler.

4. Heat ¼ cup olive oil in a large pot over medium heat. Add the onion and cook until it "sweats," or turns translucent. Do not let it brown, or burn, just become golden. Turn the heat down if it is cooking too quickly.

5. Add the garlic and oregano. Cook for 3 minutes, stirring with a wooden spoon or silicone spatula to scrape the bottom of the pot. The garlic should be fragrant.

6. Add the tomatoes. Put ½ cup water into one of the cans and swirl to loosen sauce from the sides; pour the water into the second can and swirl. Pour the water into the pot. Break the tomatoes by poking with the spoon or spatula. Simmer, uncovered for 30 minutes.

7. Season with salt and pepper. Add the milk.

8. Transfer the soup in batches to a blender or use an immersion blender right in the pot; purée the soup until very smooth.

9. Ladle the soup into oven-proof crocks. Top with a toasted bread slice. Top with 1–2 tablespoons cheese. Place the crocks onto the jelly roll pan and into the oven. If your crocks have handles, turn them in so they don't touch the sides of the oven. Broil until the cheese is melted and bubbly. Serve immediately, being careful as the crocks will be hot.

Cauliflower Cheese Soup

DAIRY ■ YIELDS 6 SERVINGS

1 large head cauliflower

1 tablespoon olive oil

1 medium onion, peeled, cut into ½-inch dice

1 teaspoon garlic powder

½ teaspoon ground white pepper

⅛ teaspoon ground mustard

2 tablespoons all-purpose flour

¼ teaspoon Worcestershire sauce

4 cups (32-ounce box) vegetable stock or broth

1 cup milk

4 ounces shredded yellow cheddar cheese

Prepare this creamy soup and a small sandwich and you've got a dynamite dinner.

1. Turn the head of cauliflower stem-side-up. Using a knife, cut the head in half. Cut the cauliflower from the core into small florets. Discard the core and leaves. Set florets aside.

2. Heat the olive oil in a large pot over medium heat. Add the onion, garlic powder, white pepper, and mustard. Sauté for 5 minutes until the onion is shiny and translucent. Stir with a wooden spoon. Add the cauliflower florets and sauté for an additional 5 minutes. The cauliflower should look a little shiny on most parts of it.

3. Sprinkle the flour into the pot. Stir until you can no longer see the flour. Add the Worcestershire sauce.

4. While stirring with the wooden spoon, loosen the browned bits from the bottom of the pot and pour in the vegetable stock. Bring to a simmer. Cover the pot and simmer for 25–30 minutes or until the cauliflower is very soft when pierced with a fork.

5. Transfer the soup in batches to a blender or use an immersion blender right in the pot; purée the soup until very smooth.

6. Pour in the milk and cheese. Stir until the cheese is melted.

7. Ladle into bowls and serve hot.

Corn Potato Chowder

MEAT, DAIRY, OR PARVE ■ YIELDS 6 SERVINGS

1 tablespoon canola oil

1 small onion, peeled and cut into ¼-inch dice

1 stalk celery, cut into ¼-inch dice

4 Yukon Gold potatoes, peeled, cut into ½-inch chunks

3 ears corn on the cob

4 cups (32-ounce box) chicken or vegetable stock or broth

fine sea salt

ground white pepper

½ cup heavy cream or soy milk

oyster crackers, optional for serving

This thick soup has a great creamy texture. Try it in the summer when corn is at its sweetest.

1. Heat the canola oil in a large soup pot over medium heat. Add the onion and celery and cook until they "sweat," or turn shiny. Do not let the onion brown, just become golden. Turn the heat down if it is cooking too quickly.

2. Add the potato chunks. Cut the corn from 2 corn cobs with a sharp knife while holding the cob at an angle. Add the corn kernels and the 2 cobs to the pot. Pour in the broth. Bring to a boil. Turn the heat down to a simmer and cook for 20–25 minutes, until potato is easily pierced with a fork. Remove and discard the cobs.

3. Transfer the soup in batches to a blender or use an immersion blender right in the pot; purée the soup until very smooth. Taste and season with salt and white pepper as necessary. Add the cream or soy milk. Stir.

4. Cut the kernels from the remaining corn cob. Ladle the soup into bowls; top with some of the corn kernels. Serve with oyster crackers if desired.

Modern Israeli Salad

PARVE ■ YIELDS 8-10 SERVINGS

4 pita breads

4 teaspoons extra-virgin olive oil

za'atar spice

2 English (hothouse) cucumbers, unpeeled

3 firm plum tomatoes

6 Israeli pickles, from a can

1 (15-ounce) can chickpeas, rinsed and drained

1 clove fresh garlic, minced

½ bunch fresh parsley leaves, chopped (about ½ cup chopped leaves)

½ teaspoon fine sea salt

½ teaspoon freshly ground black pepper

¼ cup extra-virgin olive oil

2 teaspoons fresh lemon juice (from 1 lemon)

In sleep-away camps, cans of Israeli pickles are a well-known treat. I added them along with chickpeas, the main ingredient in falafel, to round out a classic refreshing Israeli dish.

1. Preheat oven to 400°F. Line a jelly roll pan with parchment paper.

2. Arrange the pita breads on a cutting board. Drizzle 1 teaspoon olive oil on each pita and rub it into the surface of the front and back of each pita. Sprinkle the tops with za'atar. Stack the pitas by two. Cut the stacks into thin strips. Arrange in a single layer on the pan. Bake for 10 minutes, till golden and toasted.

3. Cut the cucumbers in half lengthwise. Using a measuring spoon or melon baller, scrape the seeds from the center of each half. Discard them. Place the cucumber halves cut-side-down and cut each half into 6 long strips. Then cut strips into ¼-inch pieces and place into a large mixing bowl.

4. Cut each of the tomatoes in half lengthwise. Using a spoon or melon baller, scoop out and discard the seeds. Place the tomato halves on the cutting board cut side down, and cut each half into 6 long strips. Then cut into ¼-inch pieces and place into the bowl .

5. Cut each pickle in half lengthwise and chop into ¼-inch pieces. Add to the bowl. Add the chickpeas, garlic, parsley, salt, and pepper. Mix well.

6. Drizzle in the ¼ cup olive oil and lemon juice. Toss to evenly distribute. Serve with the pita chips.

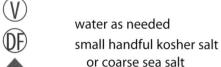

Creamy Gnocchi Pesto Salad

DAIRY OR PARVE ■ YIELDS 6 SERVINGS

water as needed

small handful kosher salt or coarse sea salt

3 tablespoons canola oil

1 tablespoon parve chicken consommé powder

2 pounds store-bought gnocchi (usually 2 packages)

4 cloves fresh garlic, chopped

2 cups fresh basil leaves, packed, about 2 ounces, stems discarded, chopped

½ cup pine nuts, plus additional for garnish

1 tablespoon low-fat mayonnaise

juice of ½ lemon

¼ teaspoon fine sea salt

½ cup good-quality extra-virgin olive oil

1 plum tomato, seeded and diced, optional

grated Parmesan, optional for dairy meals

Gnocchi are starchy Italian dumplings made from potatoes and flour. I was so excited to see prepared kosher gnocchi in the pasta aisle. They cook up in minutes and can be served with any sauce. This pesto salad is great hot if you want to serve it as a main dish, but it is just as nice over the gnocchi at room temperature and served as a variation on pasta salad.

1. Fill a large pot ¾ full of water. Add salt, canola oil, and consommé powder. Whisk to dissolve. Bring to a boil. Add the gnocchi and cook for 3–4 minutes or until they rise to the top.

2. Remove ¼ cup cooking water and set it aside. Drain the gnocchi in a colander and rinse in very cold water. Place into serving bowl and set aside.

3. Into a quart-sized container, place the chopped garlic, basil, pine nuts, reserved cooking water, mayonnaise, lemon juice, and salt. Using an immersion blender, purée until smooth. This can also be done in a food processor fitted with a metal "S" blade. With the motor running, slowly drizzle in the olive oil. Scrape down the sides of the bowl or container and pulse 2–3 times.

4. Toss the pesto over the gnocchi. Sprinkle with tomato and cheese, if using. Garnish with a handful of whole pine nuts.

Mango Brown Rice Salad

MEAT OR PARVE ■ YIELDS 6 SERVINGS

2 cups short-grain brown rice

4 cups chicken or vegetable stock or broth

2 mangoes, peeled, pitted, and cut into ½-inch dice

½ medium red onion, peeled, very finely cut into tiny dice

3 tablespoons chopped fresh cilantro leaves

1 (15-ounce) can black beans, drained and rinsed

2 tablespoons lime juice (can be bottled)

2 tablespoons extra-virgin olive oil

¾ teaspoon fine sea salt

¾ teaspoon freshly ground black pepper

Cutting a mango for the first time can be tricky. A mango has one long, flat seed in the center of the fruit and you need to cut around it. Hold the mango on your cutting board, stem end down. Place your knife about ¼-inch from the center line and cut down through the mango, trimming around the hard pit. Flip the mango around and repeat this cut on the other side. The resulting ovals of mango flesh are known as the "cheeks". Peel off the skin and cut the flesh into cubes or slices. What's left in the middle is mostly the mango seed but is a favorite snack that gets fought over in my house.

1. Place the rice and stock or broth into a pot. Bring to a boil. Cover with a tight-fitting lid and turn the heat down to a low simmer. Cook for 50 minutes. Allow the rice to stand, covered, with the heat turned off, for 10 minutes.

2. Meanwhile, in a large bowl, mix the mango, onion, cilantro, and black beans.

3. Stir in the rice. Add the lime juice, olive oil, salt, and pepper. Toss to combine well.

4. Spoon into serving bowl. Can be served warm or at room temperature.

Lox and Avocado Salad

PARVE ■ YIELDS 6 SERVINGS

2 heads Bibb or Boston lettuce, separated into individual leaves

¼ teaspoon lemon juice

1 teaspoon extra-virgin olive oil

¼ cup spicy brown mustard

1 tablespoon balsamic vinegar

2 tablespoons water

¼ pound smoked salmon, sliced

3 plum tomatoes, thinly sliced

½ small red onion, peeled, very thinly sliced

2 avocados, pitted, peeled, thinly sliced

Lox isn't just for bagels. Try it in this delightful salad that pairs it with creamy avocado and a spicy mustard dressing.

1. Place the lettuce leaves into a large bowl. Drizzle on the lemon juice and olive oil. Toss and rub into the leaves.

2. In a small bowl mix the mustard, balsamic vinegar, and water. Set aside.

3. Arrange a handful of lettuce on each plate. Tear a slice or two of smoked salmon into bite-size pieces and tuck into the lettuce. Add some tomato slices, onion, and avocado to each serving. Drizzle with the balsamic mustard.

Greek Turkey Salad

MEAT ■ YIELDS 6 SERVINGS

½ cup red wine vinegar

1½ teaspoons garlic powder

1½ teaspoons dried oregano leaves

1½ teaspoons dried basil

1 teaspoon onion powder

1 teaspoon freshly ground black pepper

1 teaspoon fine sea salt

1 teaspoon Dijon mustard

½ cup extra-virgin olive oil

1 head romaine lettuce, finely chopped

1 small English (hothouse) cucumber, peeled and cut into ½-inch dice

½ medium red onion, peeled and cut into very thin slices

½ cup sliced black olives

1 cup sliced grape tomatoes

½ pound plain or smoked store-bought turkey breast, sliced or cut into cubes

For a dairy option, leave out the turkey and crumble in some feta cheese. For a vegetarian option, toss in some cubed tofu.

1. In a quart-sized container, whisk or cover and shake the vinegar, garlic powder, oregano, basil, onion powder, pepper, salt, and mustard. Pour in the olive oil. Whisk vigorously until blended. Cover and store at room temperature.

2. Place the chopped lettuce, cucumber, onion, olives, tomatoes, and turkey into a large bowl. Toss to mix well. Add dressing to coat all the lettuce; you may have extra dressing.

3. Transfer to a salad bowl or individual plates.

Chicken Tabbouleh Salad

MEAT ■ YIELDS 6-8 SERVINGS

2 boneless, skinless chicken breasts

1 teaspoon dried parsley

1 teaspoon dried oregano leaves

½ teaspoon ground cumin

½ teaspoon fine sea salt

⅛ teaspoon chili powder

⅛ teaspoon red cayenne pepper

4½ cups water

1 (13-ounce) box, or 2½ cups, kasha, also known as buckwheat, medium granulation

4 sprigs fresh mint

½ bunch parsley, trimmed, stems discarded

½ bunch scallions (about 4), roots trimmed and discarded, each cut into 4 pieces

juice of 2 lemons, about ⅓ cup

½ cup extra-virgin olive oil

20 grape tomatoes, sliced

½ teaspoon fine sea salt

Despite its name, buckwheat is not related to wheat and is naturally gluten-free. For a vegetarian option, omit the chicken, cut up some raw firm tofu and toss the cubes into some spices. Mix with the tabbouleh. Either way, you can serve it in a bowl as a main or side dish, or wrapped in lettuce leaves for a meal on the go.

1. Preheat oven to 400°F.

2. Place the chicken breasts on a large rectangle of foil. In a small bowl, mix the parsley, oregano, cumin, salt, chili powder, and cayenne. Sprinkle this spice mixture evenly over the chicken; rub it into both sides of each breast. Fold up the foil to make a sealed packet. Place the packet onto a cookie sheet and bake for 20 minutes, or until chicken is cooked through and no longer pink in the center.

3. In a medium pot, bring 4½ cups of water to a boil.

4. Meanwhile, place the kasha into a large empty pot. Turn the heat to medium and swirl or stir the grains around for 2 minutes until they are fragrant. Pour the boiling water over the kasha. Cover the pot, remove from heat, and allow the grains to stand for 5 minutes.

5. Place the mint, parsley, and scallions into the bowl of a food processor fitted with a metal "S" blade and pulse. You can also do this by hand by chopping the herbs very well.

6. Uncover the kasha. Drag a fork through the grains in all directions to fluff them. Add the herbs and mix well.

7. Open the chicken packet; be careful not to release steam into your face. Pour the juices from the packet into the kasha. Cube the chicken and add it to the pot as well.

8. Add the lemon juice, olive oil, tomatoes, and salt. Toss well. Transfer to serving bowl.

Tex-Mex Salad

PARVE ■ YIELDS 6 SERVINGS

3 tablespoons fresh orange juice (about the juice of 1 small navel orange)

2 tablespoons fresh lime juice

1 teaspoon sugar

½ teaspoon ground cumin

¼ teaspoon fine sea salt

¼ teaspoon black pepper

⅓ cup extra-virgin olive oil

3 cups very thinly sliced iceberg lettuce

3 cups mesclun lettuce or spring mix

1 cup grape tomatoes, quartered

kernels cut from 2 uncooked ears of corn on the cob, silks removed, or 1 cup frozen kernels, thawed

1 avocado, pitted, peeled, cut into ½-inch dice

½ red bell pepper, seeded, cut into ½-inch dice

¾ cup pumpkin seeds

This salad is also fabulous with sliced steak or cooked Mexican turkey breast cubed and tossed into it. For a dairy option, crumble on feta or goat cheese.

1. In a medium bowl, whisk the orange juice, lime juice, sugar, cumin, salt, and pepper. In a steady stream, whisk in the olive oil. Set aside.

2. In a large mixing bowl, toss the iceburg and mesclun lettuces. Add the tomatoes, corn, avocado, red bell pepper, and pumpkin seeds.

3. Pour on the dressing and toss to coat the leaves.

4. Transfer to a bowl or salad plates.

Salmon Caesar Salad

PARVE ■ YIELDS 6 SERVINGS

NF
DF

1½ pounds salmon fillet, skin and pin bones removed

1 tablespoon olive oil, divided

fine sea salt

freshly ground black pepper

1 cup low-fat mayonnaise

4 anchovies, from small tin

3 cloves fresh garlic, minced

⅓ cup water

2 teaspoons lemon juice

1 head romaine lettuce

1 heaping cup store-bought croutons

Anchovies may not sound very teen-friendly, but they are the secret ingredient in all the best Caesar salad dressings. They may be "yucky" to look at but they add body and deep rich flavor to the dressing.

1. Place the salmon on a cutting board. Drizzle ½ tablespoon olive oil over one side; rub it on all surfaces. Turn the fillet over and pour remaining ½ tablespoon olive oil on the second side, rubbing it in to coat the whole side. Season both sides with salt and pepper.

2. Heat a grill pan or skillet over medium heat until very hot. Add the salmon and sear for 3 minutes on the first side and 2 minutes on the second side. Remove from pan and set aside.

3. In the bowl of a food processor fitted with a metal "S" blade, or in a quart-sized container using an immersion blender, pulse the mayonnaise, anchovies, garlic, water, and lemon juice until a smooth dressing forms. Set aside.

4. Cut the root end from the lettuce and discard. Stack the lettuce leaves in two or three piles. Slice each pile lengthwise and then roughly chop the leaves into bite-size pieces. Place them into a large serving bowl.

5. Cut the salmon into bite-size pieces and place over the lettuce.

6. Dress the salad to taste; you may have extra dressing.

7. Top with croutons and a few grinds of fresh black pepper.

(V) (NF) (DF) (GF)

Simple Salad

PARVE ■ YIELDS 6 SERVINGS

5 ounces spring mix or other lettuce

⅓ cup red wine vinegar

½ teaspoon dried basil, crushed in your palm

¼ teaspoon sugar

¼ teaspoon dried oregano leaves, crushed in your palm

¼ teaspoon fine sea salt

1 cup extra-virgin olive oil

This recipe is a blueprint for all basic salad dressings. The ratio is always 3:1 — three parts oil to one part vinegar. Choose from apple cider vinegar, red wine vinegar, balsamic vinegar, rice vinegar, or white vinegar. Your oils can vary from grapeseed oil to canola oil, walnut oil, and many others. Experiment with any spices in your spice drawer. The salad can also be embellished in dozens of ways, from avocados, to sliced onions, to fresh or dried fruit, to nuts, cheeses, seeds, beans — you are limited only by your imagination. If you want the dressing to stay emulsified, add ½ teaspoon Dijon mustard when whisking.

Always crush dried herbs in your palm to release their natural oils and aromas.

1. Place the greens into a large salad bowl.

2. In a medium bowl, whisk the red wine vinegar, basil, sugar, oregano, and salt. Whisk in the oil.

3. Lightly dress the greens; you will have extra dressing.

No Mayo Potato Salad

PARVE ■ YIELDS 8-10 SERVINGS

3 pounds small baby red-skinned or fingerling potatoes, with peel, washed well

water as needed

5 tablespoons apple cider vinegar

2 tablespoons spicy brown mustard

1 tablespoon extra-virgin olive oil

¾ teaspoon fine sea salt

½ teaspoon dried dill

¼ teaspoon freshly ground black pepper

½ medium red onion, peeled and cut into ¼-inch dice

This perfect-for-a-barbecue-or-picnic-dish is even better on the second day, when flavors have had a chance to come together.

1. Place the potatoes into a large pot. Cover with water. Bring to a boil and cook for 20 minutes or until the largest potatoes are easily pierced with a fork.

2. Meanwhile, in a small bowl whisk the vinegar, mustard, oil, salt, dill, and pepper. Set aside.

3. Drain the potatoes; cool until you are able to handle them. Cut the smaller potatoes in half and the larger ones into quarters. Place into a large bowl.

4. Add the onion and pour the vinegar mixture over the potatoes. Toss to coat well.

Honey Mustard Slaw

PARVE ■ YIELDS 6 SERVINGS

1 (1-pound) bag coleslaw mix

¼ cup low-fat mayonnaise

2 tablespoons Dijon mustard

1 tablespoon honey

2 teaspoons lemon juice

¼ teaspoon coarse or kosher salt

⅛ teaspoon dried dill

⅛ teaspoon ground cumin

If you can't find the bagged coleslaw mix, you can use ½-head red cabbage and ½-head white cabbage. Just remove the core from each, and thinly slice, or shred using the shredding disc of a food processor.

1. Place the coleslaw mix into a large bowl. Set aside.

2. In a medium bowl, whisk the mayonnaise, Dijon mustard, honey, lemon juice, salt, dill, and cumin. Pour over the cabbage and toss to coat.

3. Marinate at least 2 hours or overnight. You can use a large ziplock bag.

4. Transfer to a serving bowl.

Poultry and Meat

Mexican Chicken

MEAT ■ YIELDS 4-6 SERVINGS

NF
DF

4 boneless, skinless chicken breasts, tenders separated, each breast cut into long strips about the size of the tenders

1½ cups cornflake crumbs

3 handfuls tortilla chips, crushed by hand to make 1 cup crushed chips

1 (1.25-ounce) packet taco seasoning mix

1 tablespoon chili powder

1¾ cups (16-ounce jar) salsa, as spicy as you like

DIPPING SAUCE:

4 tablespoons margarine

⅓ cup Frank's RedHot® or other hot sauce

¼ teaspoon garlic powder

Hot and spicy with traditional buffalo wing dipping sauce, this dish will be a sure winner at your next meal.

1. Preheat oven to 350°F. Line a jelly roll pan with parchment paper. Set aside.

2. Set up a 2-part breading station. Pour the cornflake crumbs and crushed tortilla chips into a shallow dish or tin. Mix in the taco seasoning and chili powder. Stir to evenly distribute. Pour the salsa into a second shallow dish.

3. Roll 1 strip of chicken at a time in the salsa, patting it to stick. Roll in the flavored crumbs. Place onto prepared pan. Repeat with remaining chicken, including the tenders.

4. Bake, uncovered, for 20 minutes, until chicken is no longer pink in the center.

5. In the meantime, prepare the dipping sauce: In a small pot, melt the margarine. Whisk in the hot sauce and garlic powder. Remove from heat. Alternatively, you can remove from the heat and then use an immersion blender right in the pot. Allow to cool.

6. Serve the chicken strips with the dipping sauce.

Mushroom-Crusted Roast Beef

MEAT ■ YIELDS 6-8 SERVINGS

4 ounces sliced white button mushrooms

6 cloves fresh garlic

10 fresh chives

¼ cup fresh parsley leaves

⅓ cup fresh oregano leaves

½ teaspoon coarse sea salt or kosher salt

¼ teaspoon freshly ground black pepper

½ cup olive oil

1 (3-4 pound) silver tip roast beef

Roast beef is an expensive, special-occasion item, but it is good to have it in your culinary repertoire. Keep it in mind for an upscale meal, like cooking for your parents' anniversary.

1. Preheat oven to 375°F.

2. Place the mushrooms, garlic, chives, parsley, oregano, salt, pepper, and olive oil into a food processor fitted with a metal "S" blade. Pulse until a thick paste forms. Reserve ⅓ cup of this paste to spread on the roast beef after cooking.

3. Place the roast beef on a roasting rack set on a foil-lined roasting pan. Rub the mushroom paste all over the roast. Place in oven; roast, uncovered, for 1½ hours.

4. Allow the roast to rest for 10 minutes. Spread the reserved mushroom-herb mixture over the top of the roast. Slice and transfer to platter.

a culinary masterpiece

Southwest Rotisserie Chicken Wraps

MEAT ■ YIELDS 6 SERVINGS

1 whole rotisserie or roasted chicken, skin discarded, meat shredded with 2 forks

¾ cup canned black beans, drained and rinsed

1 (8.75-ounce) can whole kernel yellow corn, drained, or 1 cup frozen corn kernels, defrosted

½ small red onion, peeled, very finely chopped (about ½ cup)

½ cup fresh cilantro, stems discarded, leaves chopped

½ cup favorite bottled barbecue sauce, such as KC Masterpiece®

2 tablespoons low-fat mayonnaise

2 tablespoons parve sour cream, such as Tofutti brand Sour Supreme®

¼ teaspoon fine sea salt

¼ teaspoon freshly ground black pepper

6 (10-inch) flour tortillas

1 head Boston lettuce, leaves chopped (about 6 cups, loosely packed)

3 plum tomatoes, halved, seeded, cut into ¼-inch dice

Give your boring leftovers new life! This dish is a great way to use up leftover chicken, but it is yummy enough that I have even made a fresh roasted chicken to use in this recipe.

1. In a medium bowl, toss the shredded chicken, beans, corn, red onion, and cilantro. Set aside.

2. In a separate bowl, whisk the barbecue sauce, mayonnaise, parve sour cream, salt, and pepper. Pour the sauce over the chicken mixture and stir to mix well.

3. The tortillas are easier to roll when they are warm, so heat each one for about 10 seconds in the microwave. Lay the tortillas flat on a work surface. Top with lettuce and tomatoes. Pile on 1 cup of the chicken mixture.

4. Roll and serve.

Tater Tot® Casserole

MEAT ■ YIELDS 4-6 SERVINGS

1 pound lean ground beef

¼ cup seasoned dry breadcrumbs

2 tablespoons ketchup, plus additional for garnish

½ teaspoon garlic powder

½ teaspoon onion powder

½ teaspoon dried oregano leaves

¼ teaspoon fine sea salt

¼ teaspoon freshly ground black pepper

spicy brown mustard or deli mustard

1 (32-ounce) bag frozen Tater Tots®

fresh chives, chopped, for garnish, optional

A super-easy main with a built-in side dish. Who doesn't love Tater Tots®? Add something green to your plate and you've got a full meal.

1. Set the rack in the center of the oven. Preheat oven to 425°F.

2. Place the ground beef and breadcrumbs into a medium bowl. Add the ketchup, garlic powder, onion powder, oregano, salt, and pepper. Use your hands to combine the mixture to distribute the spices. Pat the meat into a 9-inch glass or ceramic oven-to-table baking dish.

3. Drizzle the top with the mustard.

4. Arrange a single layer of the frozen Tater Tots® over the meat mixture.

5. Bake, uncovered, on the middle rack for 25 minutes.

6. Turn the oven to broil and broil the casserole for 3 minutes, until the Tater Tots® are golden brown.

7. Garnish with a drizzle of ketchup and, if desired, chopped chives.

Schwarma Chicken

MEAT ■ YIELDS 4 SERVINGS

2 tablespoons ground cumin

1 tablespoon ground coriander

1 tablespoon garlic powder

1 tablespoon onion powder

2 teaspoons paprika

1 teaspoon turmeric

1 teaspoon ground cinnamon

½ teaspoon fine sea salt

½ teaspoon freshly ground black pepper

4 boneless, skinless chicken breasts

1 large red onion, peeled, cut into thin strips

juice of 1½ lemons

½ cup extra-virgin olive oil

2 tablespoons canola oil

salad or pita for serving

You can make this recipe using lamb cubes for a more authentic schwarma. You can cook the lamb cubes the same way as the chicken or skewer them and pan sear the skewers.

1. In a small container, jar, or ziplock bag, mix the cumin, coriander, garlic powder, onion powder, paprika, turmeric, cinnamon, salt, and pepper.

2. Remove the tenders from the chicken cutlets and cut each tender into 3 chunks. Cut each chicken cutlet into 3 strips lengthwise and then each strip into 3–4 chunks. Place into a mixing bowl or large container. Add the onion strips and the lemon juice. Pour in olive oil and 2 tablespoons of the spice blend. Mix well. Set aside to marinate for 30 minutes.

3. Heat the canola oil in a very large skillet. Get it very hot. Add the chicken and onions in a single layer. Don't crowd the pan; cook in batches if necessary. Cook until golden brown and onions are caramelized. Flip each piece of chicken. Sprinkle on 2 more tablespoons of the spice mixture. Cook on the second side for a few minutes longer until the chicken is cooked through and no longer pink in the center. Shake the pan as the chicken sautés.

4. Remove to a plate or platter. Serve over salad or in a pita.

Ellie's Onion-Crusted Chicken

MEAT ■ YIELDS 6-8 SERVINGS

½ cup horseradish sauce

½ cup honey mustard
(I like Honeycup® or
Woebers® brand)

1 (6-ounce) can French's®
fried onions

8 bone-in chicken parts,
with skin (thighs, breasts,
and/or legs)

My cousin Ellie Langer shared this great recipe with me. Her house of 20-somethings gave it two thumbs up for its great taste, ease, heat, and crunch. To retain that crunch, reheat uncovered.

Horseradish sauce is a creamy white mayonnaise sauce that has plenty of kick! It is usually found near the mustards, ketchups, and sauces. There are numerous kosher certified brands.

1. Preheat oven to 350°F. Line a jelly roll pan with parchment paper. Set aside.

2. In a small bowl, whisk the horseradish sauce and the honey mustard. Transfer the sauce to a shallow plate or pan.

3. Pour the fried onions into a second shallow plate or pan.

4. Dip the skin side of each chicken part in the sauce and then dip into the fried onion. If using legs, roll around all surfaces. Place coated chicken on prepared pan.

5. Bake, uncovered, for 1 hour 30 minutes, until chicken is no longer pink in the middle.

6. Using tongs, transfer the chicken to a bowl or platter.

Amalfi Chicken

MEAT ■ YIELDS 6-8 SERVINGS

3 small red onions, peeled, cut into ½-inch slices

2 sprigs fresh basil

8 bone-in chicken parts (legs, thighs, and/or breasts)

½ teaspoon fine sea salt

½ teaspoon dried oregano leaves

¼ teaspoon powdered lemonade mix

⅛ teaspoon ground white pepper

2 plum tomatoes, cut into ½-inch slices

2 lemons, thinly sliced

1 ounce (15 sprigs) fresh thyme

coarse sea salt or kosher salt

This dish was inspired by the mouthwatering citrus dishes served on the Amalfi coast in Southern Italy.

Don't use diet lemonade mix — in this dish it leaves a weird aftertaste.

1. Preheat oven to 400°F.

2. Line the bottom of a 9-by-13-inch baking pan with the red onion slices. Place the basil leaves over the onions. Crush the basil stems in your palm and place them in the pan as well. Arrange the chicken skin side up on the basil.

3. In a small bowl or ramekin, mix the salt, oregano, lemonade mix, and white pepper. Sprinkle the seasoning over the chicken, rubbing it into each piece. Stand the tomato and lemon slices between the chicken parts. Slip any extras under the chicken. Toss the thyme sprigs over the top of the dish and tuck a few underneath as well for the perfume.

4. Bake, uncovered, for 50 minutes.

5. Transfer to a platter. Sprinkle with a pinch of coarse sea salt.

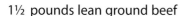

Pastrami Burgers

MEAT ■ YIELDS 6 BURGERS

1½ pounds lean ground beef

½ teaspoon dried oregano leaves

¼ teaspoon garlic powder

¼ teaspoon onion powder

¼ teaspoon fine sea salt

⅛ cup favorite barbecue sauce (I like KC Masterpiece® brand)

high-heat or professional cooking spray

¼ pound sliced pastrami

hamburger buns

Yum, yum, and yum. For meat lovers it doesn't get any better than this. By slowly rendering out the fat, you crisp up the pastrami and intensify its flavor.

1. Place the ground beef, oregano, garlic powder, onion powder, salt, and barbecue sauce into a large bowl. With your hands, work the spices into the meat. Divide the meat into 6 portions and with wet hands form patties.

2. Spray a grill pan or skillet with high-heat cooking spray. Heat over medium until very hot but not smoking.

3. Place the patties into the pan and sear the burgers, 3–4 minutes per side for medium. Remove the burgers to a plate as they are done.

4. In the pan drippings, lay the strips of pastrami and allow them to sizzle, shrivel, and render out their fat. This will make them a little crispy; do not move the pastrami around.

5. Serve the burgers on buns, topped with the pastrami.

Meatball Subs

MEAT ■ YIELDS 6 SERVINGS

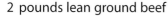

2 pounds lean ground beef

3 large eggs

1½ teaspoons garlic powder

1 teaspoon onion powder

1 teaspoon dried oregano leaves, crushed in your palm

1 teaspoon fine sea salt

¼ teaspoon red cayenne pepper

olive oil

2 red bell peppers, seeded and thinly sliced

2 onions, peeled, halved, and thinly sliced

1 (26-28-ounce) jar favorite pizza or marinara sauce

¼ cup water

6 hoagie or sub rolls

To make this a more healthful dish, you can use half ground turkey and half ground beef. Either way, use 80% lean ground beef.

1. Select a large skillet that has a lid. Set aside.

2. In a large bowl, mix the beef, eggs, garlic powder, onion powder, oregano, salt, and cayenne. Use both hands to really combine all the spices into the meat. Using a medium (size 30) scoop, or by hand, form 24 golf ball-sized meatballs, rolling very well between your wet palms.

3. Pour about 2–3 tablespoons olive oil into the bottom of the skillet, making sure it coats the bottom. Heat the olive oil over medium. Add a single layer of meatballs, using tongs to turn them to brown on all sides. Remove each meatball when done and add others as space opens up.

4. Wipe out the skillet and add 1 tablespoon olive oil in the pan. Heat oil and add the red peppers and onions. Sauté until limp, about 5–6 minutes. Add the meatballs back into the skillet and cover with the pizza or marinara sauce. Pour ¼ cup water into the jar. Swirl to loosen the sauce from the sides and add it to the meatballs. Cover the skillet and cook over medium heat for 15 minutes.

5. Scoop 4 meatballs with some of the peppers, onions, and sauce into each hoagie roll. Place on plate or platter.

NF

DF

GF

3 jalapeño peppers

10 cloves fresh garlic, peeled

2 scallions, roots trimmed and discarded, each cut into 4 pieces

¾ cup canola oil

½ cup ketchup

1 teaspoon paprika

1 teaspoon sugar

½ filet split (1-2 pounds)

high heat or professional cooking spray

1 scallion, roots trimmed and discarded, thinly sliced on the diagonal, for garnish

Firecracker Beef

MEAT ■ YIELDS 6 SERVINGS

Pour a tall glass of water! This one explodes with heat and flavor. Wear disposable gloves to keep your hands from burning when working with jalapeños. Make sure not to touch your eyes, nose, or mouth, as the oils will burn them. When you are finished, wash your hands with soap and water.

For this recipe you can substitute one pound of skirt steak sliced against the grain. It is great served with the Toasted Sesame Rice (see page 166).

1. Cut off and discard the stem of each jalapeño. Cut each pepper in half lengthwise, and then into 4 chunks, with the seeds. Place into the bowl of a food processor fitted with a metal "S" blade. Add the garlic, scallions, oil, ketchup, paprika, and sugar. Pulse until a smooth sauce forms.

2. Cut the filet split in half lengthwise. Then, slice crosswise into ½-inch-thick strips to make bite-size pieces. Place the strips into a large bowl. Add the sauce and toss to coat.

3. Spray a large frying pan or skillet with nonstick cooking spray. Heat over medium-high until hot but not smoking. Add the beef in a single layer. Do this in batches if necessary. Cook for 3 minutes until the meat begins to caramelize and brown. Using tongs, turn each piece and cook for 3 minutes on the second side.

4. Serve over rice or couscous. Garnish with sliced scallions.

Sticky Orange Herb-Roasted Chicken

MEAT ■ YIELDS 4-6 SERVINGS

1 whole chicken, legs tied

fine sea salt

freshly ground black pepper

BASTING SAUCE:

6 tablespoons orange marmalade (I like Smuckers® brand)

2 tablespoons teriyaki sauce

½ teaspoon dried rosemary, crumbled

½ teaspoon dried thyme

½ teaspoon garlic powder

To clean the chicken, try using a strawberry huller to grab the feathers. Don't worry about getting every last feather, they are easier to remove once the chicken is roasted. If you don't have a rack to cook chicken on, get one! But in the meantime, roll a length of aluminum foil into a stick. Bring the ends together to form a circle. Place the circle on the lined jelly roll pan and set the chicken on it. It will elevate the chicken out of its own juices and allow the skin to crisp up, even on the bottom. Tying the legs will keep them from flopping open and tearing the skin. You can use a supermarket twist-tie if you don't have kitchen twine or a silicone band.

1. Move the oven rack to the lowest position. Preheat oven to 375°F.

2. Line a jelly roll pan with aluminum foil for easy cleanup. Set a rack (see note) on the pan. Set aside.

3. Season the chicken with salt and pepper on the front and back. Place on the rack, breast side up.

4. Prepare the basting sauce: In a small bowl, mix the marmalade, teriyaki sauce, rosemary, thyme, and garlic powder. Using a silicone or pastry brush, brush an even layer of sauce all over the chicken. Wipe up any sauce that dripped on the pan, to keep it from burning. Bake 20 minutes. Remove the chicken from the oven and baste with sauce again. Return to the oven and bake for 15 minutes.

5. Baste for the third time and bake for 15 minutes. Baste with the remaining marinade and bake for the final 15 minutes. The chicken should be golden and the skin should look crisp. Remove from oven and allow the chicken to rest for 10 minutes.

6. Transfer to serving platter and carve.

Thai Chicken Burgers

MEAT ■ YIELDS 6 SERVINGS

CURRY MAYONNAISE:

¼ cup mayonnaise, can be low-fat

2 tablespoons creamy peanut butter, can be low-fat

½ teaspoon curry powder

THAI CHICKEN BURGERS:

2 pounds ground chicken

¼ cup panko breadcrumbs

1 large egg

¼ teaspoon dried basil

¼ teaspoon garlic powder

¼ teaspoon fine sea salt

⅛ teaspoon freshly ground black pepper (5 turns of peppermill)

⅛ teaspoon ground ginger

high heat or professional cooking spray

6 hamburger buns

1 avocado, pitted, peeled, and sliced

6 fresh basil leaves

If you are buying the ground chicken from a butcher, ask for a mix of dark and white ground chicken. If you can't find ground chicken, simply place 6 boneless, skinless chicken breasts (cutlets) into a food processor fitted with a metal "S" blade and, using a few 1-second pulses, chop the chicken; just don't grind it too finely.

1. Prepare the curry mayonnaise: In a small bowl, mix the mayonnaise, peanut butter, and curry powder. Set aside.

2. Place the ground chicken and breadcrumbs into a medium bowl. Add the egg, basil, garlic powder, salt, pepper, and ginger. Mix by hand. Wet your hands to keep the chicken from sticking, and make 6 big patties. You want them to be flatter than a typical hamburger so they will cook fast and have less chance to dry out.

3. Spray a grill pan or skillet with nonstick cooking spray. Heat the pan until hot but not smoking. Cook the chicken burgers 3–4 minutes per side, until no longer pink in the center. Set aside.

4. Spread the curry mayonnaise on the bottom half of each bun. Top with a chicken burger, a few slices of avocado, and a basil leaf. Cover each burger with the top half of the bun and place on a platter.

Teriyaki Mushroom Chicken

MEAT ■ YIELDS 4 SERVINGS

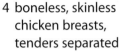

4 boneless, skinless chicken breasts, tenders separated

10 ounces sliced button or crimini mushrooms

½ cup teriyaki sauce (I like Kikkoman®)

3 tablespoons rice vinegar

4 teaspoons roasted or toasted sesame oil

2 teaspoons ground ginger

8 cloves fresh garlic, minced

2 tablespoons olive oil

fresh chives, for garnish

This dish is great served over simple steamed white or brown rice.

1. Cut each chicken breast in half lengthwise. Cut each strip crosswise into ½-inch-thick strips, to make bite-size pieces. Cut the tenders into bite-size pieces as well. Transfer to a large ziplock bag along with the sliced mushrooms.

2. In a medium bowl, whisk the teriyaki sauce, rice vinegar, sesame oil, ginger, and garlic. Pour into the bag. Seal the bag. Massage into the chicken pieces and allow to marinate in the refrigerator for at least a few hours or overnight.

3. Bring the chicken to room temperature. Heat the olive oil in a large skillet. Remove the chicken and mushrooms from the bag, discarding the marinade, and sauté in a single layer for 4–5 minutes, stirring to cook all sides, until the chicken is cooked through. Do not crowd the pan. Depending on the size of your pan, you may need to do this in two batches.

4. Transfer to serving plate or platter.

5. Garnish with fresh chives.

Apricot Sesame Roast

MEAT ■ YIELDS 6-8 SERVINGS

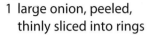

1 large onion, peeled, thinly sliced into rings

3 pound California, French, or square beef roast

1 (12-ounce) jar apricot jelly

1 cup hoisin sauce

6 cloves fresh garlic, minced

2 teaspoons roasted or toasted sesame oil

This meat is perfect for a Shabbos roast and couldn't be easier. These cuts of meat will slice nicely and not shred or fall apart like brisket or pot roast.

1. Preheat oven to 350°F.

2. Select a baking dish that will hold the roast snugly.

3. Scatter half the onion rings in a single layer in the dish. Set the meat on the onions. Scatter the remaining onions over the top of the roast.

4. In a medium bowl, whisk the apricot jelly, hoisin sauce, garlic, and sesame oil. Pour over the meat. Cover with foil and bake for 2 hours 15 minutes.

5. Allow the meat to cool for 10 minutes before thinly slicing. Serve with pan juices.

Homemade Chickies

MEAT ■ YIELDS 4 SERVINGS

2 cups thin salted pretzel sticks, pressed into measuring cup to fit

2 cups store brand, parve, Captain Crunch® cereal

canola oil

4 boneless, skinless chicken breasts, tenders removed, sliced in half horizontally through the thickness

1 cup low-fat mayonnaise

1 tablespoon honey

2 cloves fresh garlic, minced

¼ teaspoon garlic powder

2 tablespoons water

2 (16-inch) French or Italian breads, halved and split horizontally

¼ head iceberg lettuce, shredded

2 firm plum tomatoes, very thinly sliced

2 sour pickles, very thinly sliced into rounds

If you are lucky enough to live in or near Teaneck, NJ, then without a doubt you have heard of Chickies, a hole-in-the-wall that serves the greatest chicken sandwiches and has lines out the door at all hours of the night to back this claim. It is my kids' favorite treat and if we ever drive within 10 miles of the place we are drawn to it as if by a homing device. For those of you not lucky enough to live nearby, here is my homemade version that holds my family over between Chickies runs.

1. In the bowl of a food processor fitted with the metal "S" blade, pulse the pretzels until mostly crushed. Add the cereal and pulse again until it is a breading with just small bits of pretzel visible for texture.

2. Transfer the coating to a shallow pan or platter.

3. Pour canola oil to come up 2 inches on a large pot or high-sided skillet. Heat over medium.

4. Bread the chicken in the cereal/pretzel coating by laying the chicken into the pan and pressing in the coating. Repeat with remaining chicken.

5. Test the oil to make sure it is ready. Add a small pinch of the remaining coating to the oil: if it is hot enough it should bubble around the coating; if coating turns brown immediately, the oil is too hot and heat should be turned down. Carefully place 2–3 pieces of chicken into the hot oil. Do not crowd the pan. Allow to fry for 2–3 minutes until golden brown. With metal tongs, carefully turn each cutlet and fry on the second side until it is golden as well.

6. Remove to a paper towel-lined plate or tin and repeat with remaining chicken.

7. In a quart-sized container, whisk the mayonnaise, honey, garlic, garlic powder, and water until smooth and runny. Spread this sauce generously on the 4 bread halves.

8. On each bread half, place 2 pieces of chicken, lettuce, tomatoes, and pickles. Serve warm.

Garlic Rosemary Filet Split

MEAT ■ YIELDS 6 SERVINGS

1½ pounds filet split

6 cloves fresh garlic

1 tablespoon dried rosemary, crumbled in your palm

3 tablespoons dark brown sugar

2 tablespoons parve Worcestershire sauce

2 tablespoons balsamic vinegar

⅓ cup canola oil

¼ cup soy sauce

high heat or professional cooking spray

You can substitute dried thyme for the rosemary for a slightly different flavor.

Filet split is a very thin cut of meat and will cook very quickly. You can substitute with shoulder London broil, but it is thicker and will need to cook 10–15 minutes per side.

1. Place the meat into a large ziplock bag. Set aside.

2. Place the garlic, rosemary, brown sugar, Worcestershire sauce, balsamic, oil, and soy sauce into a quart-sized container. Using an immersion blender, mix the ingredients until a smooth marinade forms. Pour into the bag and seal the bag. Massage the marinade into the meat. Allow to marinate for at least 10 minutes.

3. Spray a grill pan or large skillet with nonstick cooking spray. Heat the pan over medium heat, until very hot but not smoking. Remove the meat from the marinade. Discard the marinade. Set the meat down into the pan. Allow it to sear without moving it at all for 8 minutes for medium doneness. Using tongs, turn the steak and cook for an additional 6-8 minutes on the other side. Remove the meat from the pan. Set it on a cutting board. Allow meat to stand for 10 minutes before slicing on the diagonal.

4. Transfer sliced steak to a platter.

A note about Worcestershire sauce:

True Worcestershire sauce contains anchovies. If the kosher certification mark stands alone, then the percentage of anchovies is less than 1.6% of the whole product. Many rabbinical authorites say that this is okay to use with meat.

If the kosher certification on the label has a fish notation next to it, the level exceeds 1.6%; do not use it in meat dishes.

Salami and Egg Scramble

MEAT ■ YIELDS 1 SERVING

3 slices salami

2 large eggs, lightly beaten

fine sea salt

freshly ground black
pepper

Ton of studying to do? No time to cook but need a protein burst? Whip up this lunch or dinner in 3 minutes flat!

1. Heat a medium nonstick skillet over medium heat. Add the salami. Allow it to cook so that the fat renders out and the salami begins to shrivel, about 2 minutes.

2. Add the eggs and scramble as they cook.

3. Season with salt and pepper.

4. Transfer to a plate and serve hot.

Fish, Pasta, and Dairy

delicious & healthy

Pesto Salmon

PARVE ■ YIELDS 4 SERVINGS

1 pound salmon fillet, without skin, pin bones removed

fine sea salt

freshly ground black pepper

1 cup fresh basil leaves (the picked-off leaves of a medium bunch)

3 cloves fresh garlic, sliced

½ cup pine nuts

¾ cup extra-virgin olive oil

½ teaspoon fine sea salt

¼ teaspoon freshly ground black pepper

With little fuss, this fast-cooking dish packs a wallop of good health on your plate. High in Omega-3 fatty acids and Vitamin D, salmon is brain food. It is great for dinner on a night you are cramming for exams.

1. Preheat oven to 375°F. Line a jelly roll pan with aluminum foil. Place the salmon in the center of the pan. Season with salt and pepper. Set aside.

2. Place the basil leaves into a quart-sized container. Add the sliced garlic and pine nuts. Using an immersion blender, pulse until pesto is puréed. You can also do this in a food processor fitted with the metal "S" blade. With the machine running, drizzle in the olive oil. Add ½ teaspoon salt and ¼ teaspoon pepper; process again.

3. Reserve ¼ cup of the pesto to serve with the fish. Using a pastry brush, gently brush the fish with the remaining pesto.

4. Bake, uncovered, for 25 minutes.

5. Transfer the salmon to a platter. Serve with the reserved pesto.

Layered Mushroom Ziti

DAIRY ■ YIELDS 10-12 SERVINGS

1 (16-ounce) box ziti

kosher or coarse salt

water as needed

1 medium onion, peeled, cut into chunks

4 cloves fresh garlic, coarsely chopped

2 (10-ounce) boxes button mushrooms, cleaned

2 tablespoons olive oil

½ teaspoon fine sea salt

½ teaspoon freshly ground black pepper

4 cups jarred marinara sauce

1 cup shredded mozzarella cheese

1 cup shredded cheddar cheese

2 cups ricotta cheese

2 tablespoons grated Parmesan cheese

2 tablespoons grated Romano cheese

Often there is a layer of beef in non-kosher baked ziti. In this recipe, mushrooms are chopped and sautéed to simulate that deep meaty flavor in a dish that you and your friends will go crazy for. If you can't find Romano cheese, just use double the amount of Parmesan. The better quality sauces are often sold in 25-ounce jars, so you may need a second jar.

1. Preheat oven to 375°F.

2. Cook the ziti in a large pot of salted, rapidly boiling water according to the package instructions, until al dente. Drain and rinse under cold water to stop the cooking process. Set aside.

3. Meanwhile, place half the onion and garlic into a food processor fitted with metal "S" blade. Pulse a few times until evenly chopped. Add one box of mushrooms. Pulse until finely chopped. Remove the contents to a bowl. Add the second box of mushrooms with the remaining onion and garlic and process until finely chopped. Add them to the bowl.

4. In the empty ziti pot, heat the olive oil over medium heat. Transfer the chopped mushrooms to the pot and sauté for about 15 minutes to remove the moisture from the mushrooms. This will give them a meaty flavor. Add the salt and pepper. Stir.

5. Arrange a single layer of the cooked ziti in a 9-by-13-inch oven-to-table or Pyrex pan. You can line them up in rows if you want to be fancy. Spread 1 cup of the marinara over the ziti layer. Top with an even sprinkling of all the mozzarella. Spread half the mushroom mixture over the cheese. Top with 1 cup of sauce. Sprinkle on all of the cheddar cheese and arrange the rest of the ziti on the cheddar. Top with remaining mushrooms and remaining cups of sauce.

6. Spread an even layer of the ricotta over the top using a spoon or offset spatula. Sprinkle on the Parmesan and Romano cheeses.

7. Bake, uncovered, for 40 minutes, until cheese is bubbly and starting to brown. Serve hot.

Banana Buttermilk Pancakes with Strawberry Sauce

DAIRY ■ YIELDS 8 PANCAKES

STRAWBERRY SAUCE:
- 1 pound fresh strawberries
- 1½ cups sugar
- 2 tablespoons fresh lemon juice (the juice of about 1 lemon)

PANCAKES:
- 1 cup all-purpose flour
- 2 tablespoons sugar
- 1 teaspoon baking powder
- ½ teaspoon baking soda
- ¼ teaspoon fine sea salt
- 2-3 tablespoons canola oil for skillet
- 1 cup buttermilk
- 3 tablespoons milk
- 1 large egg
- 2 tablespoons melted butter
- 1 ripe but firm banana, very thinly sliced
- high heat or professional cooking spray

These buttermilk pancakes are the lightest and fluffiest I have ever had. I know you will love them. You can make the strawberry sauce in advance and keep it in the fridge for up to a week. You can try the sauce with other berries as well, like blueberries or raspberries; you may need to strain the seeds or pulp from those. You can keep the pancakes warm on a cookie sheet in a 200°F oven until ready to serve.

1. Remove the stem from each strawberry. Using a very small (one-eighth teaspoon) measuring spoon or a strawberry huller, remove and discard the hull. Place the strawberries into a medium-large pot. Using an immersion blender right in the pot, purée the strawberries. This can also be done in a food processor fitted with a metal "S" blade; purée and transfer to the pot.

2. Add the sugar and lemon juice. Stir. Place over medium heat. Bring to a boil, and then turn the heat down slightly and allow the mixture to simmer, uncovered, for 20 minutes. Check often to make sure it is not bubbling over. If it does, lift the pot and lower the heat slightly. Remove from heat and set aside to cool.

3. Meanwhile, in a medium bowl, using a sifter, sift the flour, sugar, baking powder, baking soda, and salt. If you don't have a sifter, pass it though a metal strainer.

4. Coat a nonstick skillet or griddle with canola oil. Heat over medium.

5. When you are ready to cook, make a well in the center of the dry ingredients. Add the buttermilk, milk, egg, and melted butter. Using a few strokes, mix with silicone spatula or wooden spoon until blended. It is ok if there are some lumps. Have all the flour incorporated, but make sure not to overmix or the batter will toughen.

6. Using a ⅓-cup measure, carefully pour 3–4 portions of batter Into the hot skillet. Arrange groups of banana slices on the batter, 3–4 per pancake. They should touch but not overlap. Cook for 2 minutes or until surface is bubbly. Using a metal spatula, flip each pancake and cook for another 2 minutes until golden brown. Spray the pan with nonstick cooking spray and repeat with remaining batter and bananas. Serve with strawberry sauce.

Tuna Niçoise Wrap

PARVE ■ YIELDS 4 SERVINGS

NF
DF

3 large eggs

water as needed

20 Niçoise, Kalamata, or Gaeta olives

12 Boston or romaine lettuce leaves

20 grape tomatoes

2 (5-ounce) cans tuna, packed in oil

2 cloves fresh garlic, minced

⅓ cup low-fat mayonnasie

½ teaspoon lemon juice

2 teaspoons extra-virgin olive oil

4 large flour tortillas

Canned tuna can get to be a bit boring, so let this recipe liven it up to a gourmet level. Use the tuna packed in oil for a moist result.

1. Place the eggs into a small pot that holds them in a single layer. Cover with cold water. Bring to a boil over medium heat. Cover the pot. Remove from heat and allow the eggs to stand for 15 minutes. Run the eggs under cold water. When cool enough to handle, roll them on the counter to crack the shells in a few places. Peel the eggs and place into a medium bowl, rinsing to make sure there is no shell left.

2. Meanwhile, smack each olive with the palm of your hand on your cutting board to pop the pit out; discard the pits. Chop all the olives and set aside. Stack the lettuce leaves; cut out the stem if using romaine. Thinly slice the lettuce to make shreds. Set aside. Slice the grape tomatoes, set aside.

3. Open and drain the cans of tuna. Place the tuna into a medium bowl. Using a fork, mix in the garlic, mayonnaise, lemon juice, and olive oil.

4. Lay the tortillas on your work surface. Place a line of lettuce down the center of each tortilla. Slice the eggs and arrange 3 egg slices on the lettuce. Top with tuna. Sprinkle on the olives and tomatoes.

5. Working with one tortilla at a time, roll in the sides of the tortilla. Roll up from the bottom, pushing the filling in as you roll. Repeat with remaining tortillas. Cut each wrap on the diagonal.

6. To serve, stand 2 halves on each plate.

Falafel Veggie Burgers

PARVE ■ YIELDS 8 SERVINGS

6-8 sprigs fresh cilantro

½ bunch fresh parsley (about 25 sprigs)

1 small red onion, peeled and quartered

1 (15-ounce) can small white beans, drained and rinsed

1 (15-ounce) can chickpeas or garbanzo beans, drained and rinsed

6 tablespoons all-purpose flour

1½ teaspoons baking powder

1 teaspoon ground cumin

1 teaspoon garlic powder

½ teaspoon fine sea salt

¼ teaspoon red cayenne pepper

olive oil

8 pita breads or buns, warmed

store-bought chummos

A meal in minutes and vegan to boot! Chickpeas and white beans are an easy source of protein and fiber, and are low in fat. If friends or family members are arriving home for dinner on different schedules, store uncooked, shaped patties in the fridge and just cook them up as you need them.

1. Cut off and discard the bottom stems of the cilantro and parsley. Wash the sprigs well and squeeze dry. Place them into the bowl of a food processor fitted with a metal "S" blade.

2. Add the onion and pulse 3–4 times. Add the white beans. Pulse until almost smooth.

3. Add the chickpeas and pulse a few times, using on-off pulses, leaving a little texture from the chickpeas. Empty mixture into a large mixing bowl.

4. Add the flour, baking powder, cumin, garlic powder, salt, and cayenne pepper. Mix well. With wet hands, form into 8 patties. Set aside.

5. In a medium skillet, heat 2 tablespoons olive oil. Add 2–3 patties at a time, being careful not to crowd the pan. Sear for 2 minutes per side, until golden brown. Add 1–2 tablespoons more oil if necessary when flipping and between batches; just make sure you allow the oil to heat before adding the next patties.

6. Serve with chummos on buns or in pitas.

great source of fiber

Pineapple-Maple Glazed Salmon

PARVE ■ YIELDS 6 SERVINGS

6 (6-ounce) salmon fillets, without skin, pin bones removed

¼ cup maple syrup (NOT pancake syrup)

¼ cup crushed pineapple, from a small can, squeezed dry

3 tablespoons soy sauce

2 tablespoons Dijon mustard

1 tablespoon olive oil

2 cloves fresh garlic, minced

Three minutes of active prep time plus fifteen in the oven yields you a gourmet, healthful dish. Salmon is a fish we should all be eating more of. Feel free to experiment with the gamier wild salmon; it can yield even more health benefits than farm-raised.

1. Preheat oven to 375°F.

2. Rinse the salmon and place it on a small parchment-lined jelly roll pan. Pat dry with paper towels.

3. In a medium bowl, whisk the maple syrup, pineapple, soy sauce, mustard, olive oil, and garlic.

4. Pour over the salmon and bake, uncovered, for 15 minutes.

5. Transfer to serving platter. Drizzle with pan juices. Serve hot or at room temperature.

Eggplant Parmesan

DAIRY ■ YIELDS 9 SERVINGS

2 medium, 3-inch diameter, Italian eggplants (1½ pounds total), peeled and sliced into ¼-inch rounds

coarse or kosher salt

2 cups all-purpose flour

4 large eggs, lightly beaten

4 cups (8 ounces) panko breadcrumbs

¼ cup grated Parmesan cheese

1 teaspoon dried oregano leaves

1 teaspoon garlic powder

½ teaspoon dried parsley

½ teaspoon dried basil

2 jars favorite marinara sauce

1 cup fat-free ricotta cheese

16 ounces shredded mozzarella

Baking the eggplant in this recipe takes a classic and lightens it up a bit. It is a fantastic dish if having a bunch of friends over, since it feeds a crowd.

1. Preheat oven to 450°F. Line two jelly roll pans with parchment paper. Set aside.

2. Place the eggplant slices in a single layer on a large cookie sheet or large cutting board. Sprinkle with coarse salt, top with paper towels, and allow to stand for 20 minutes while the salt extracts the bitterness from the eggplant.

3. Rinse the eggplant slices and pat dry.

4. Set up a 3-part breading station, using 3 tins or shallow containers: Put the flour into the first container and beaten eggs into the second. In the third, mix the panko breadcrumbs, Parmesan, oregano, garlic powder, parsley, and basil.

5. Dredge an eggplant slice in the flour, shaking off excess. Dip both sides into the egg and then into the flavored breadcrumbs. Place in a single layer on the prepared parchment-lined pans.

6. Bake the eggplant for 8 minutes. Carefully flip each slice and bake for 8 minutes on the other side.

7. Spread a layer of plain marinara into a 9-by-13-inch baking pan or oven-to-table-casserole dish. Arrange a layer of eggplant, slightly overlapping, on the sauce.

8. In a medium bowl, mix the ricotta with the second jar of marinara sauce. Spread a layer of this sauced ricotta over the eggplant. Top with a sprinkling of half the mozzarella.

9. Repeat for a second layer with all the remaining ingredients: plain sauce, eggplant, ricotta sauce, and cheese.

10. Bake in the oven, covered, for 10 minutes, and then uncovered for 15 minutes or until hot and bubbly. Serve hot.

Amazing
Egg Salad Sandwiches

PARVE ■ YIELDS 4 SANDWICHES

8 large eggs

water to cover

1 tablespoon olive oil

1 medium onion, peeled, cut into ¼-inch dice

6 large crimini mushrooms, brushed clean, thinly sliced

2½ tablespoons low-fat mayonnaise

1½ tablespoons chopped fresh dill

¼ teaspoon fine sea salt

¼ teaspoon freshly ground black pepper

4 Boston lettuce leaves

8 slices whole-grain bread

Don't overcook the eggs or the yolks will turn a funky shade of green. The eggs will still be safe to eat but they will look a little funny.

1. Place the eggs into a pot that holds them in a single layer. Cover with cold water. Bring to a boil over medium heat. Cover the pot. Remove from heat and allow the eggs to stand for 15 minutes. Run the eggs under cold water. When cool enough to handle, roll them on the counter to crack the shells in a few places. Peel the eggs and place into a medium bowl, rinsing to make sure there is no shell left.

2. Meanwhile, in a medium pan, heat the olive oil. Sauté the onion until it is translucent and starts to turn golden, about 5–6 minutes. Add the mushrooms and sauté for another 4–5 minutes until the mushrooms are limp.

3. With a potato masher or back of a large fork, break and mash the eggs. Add the sautéed mushrooms and onions. Mix in the mayonnaise, dill, salt, and pepper. Stir well.

4. Toast the bread slices to desired doneness.

5. Arrange a lettuce leaf on 4 of the toasted slices. Top with egg salad and the remaining toast to make sandwiches. You can secure with toothpicks. Transfer the sandwiches to plates or a platter.

Fish Tacos

PARVE ■ YIELDS 4 TACOS

FISH PACKET:
1 pound (a large rectanglar piece) white flaky fish such as mahi mahi, cod, or halibut
½ fresh lemon
  fresh cilantro leaves
4 soft corn or flour tortillas
3 leaves green cabbage, shredded
1 avocado, peeled, pit removed, diced

PICO DE GALLO:
  handful fresh cilantro leaves
2 plum tomatoes, diced
1 jalapeño pepper, seeded, minced
½ small onion, peeled, cut into ¼-inch dice
¼ teaspoon fine sea salt
¼ teaspoon freshly ground black pepper

LIME MAYONNAISE:
⅓ cup low-fat mayonnaise
1 teaspoon fresh lime juice

Fish tacos originated in Mexico's Baja Peninsula and are hugely popular in California. This recipe is for the oven but can easily be done outdoors on a grill, grilling the fish 4–5 minutes per side.

The pico de gallo is a nice raw salsa that can be used in many ways, so be sure to make extra. Serve some with chips, mixed into a salad, or over any fish, chicken breast, burger, or steak.

Keep your hands from being burned when working with jalapeños by wearing disposable gloves. Make sure not to touch your eyes, nose, or mouth, as the oils will burn them. When you are finished, wash your hands with soap and water.

1. Preheat oven to 375°F.

2. Cut a large rectangle of aluminum foil. Place the fish in the center of the foil. Squeeze the lemon half over the fish, removing any pits, and scatter on a few cilantro leaves. Seal the foil packet, place on a cookie sheet, and bake for 10–15 minutes, depending on thickness of the fish.

3. Stack the tortillas, wrap in foil, and place into the oven to warm.

4. Prepare the Pico de Gallo: Mince a small handful of cilantro leaves to yield 1 tablespoon minced leaves. Place into a medium bowl. Add the tomatoes, jalapeño, onion, salt, and pepper. Mix well. Set aside.

5. Prepare the Lime Mayonnaise: In a small bowl, mix the mayonnaise with the lime juice.

6. Remove the tortillas from the oven. Spread some of the lime mayonnaise on one half of each tortilla. Remove the fish from the oven and carefully open the packet. Using a fork, flake the fish. Place one-fourth of the fish over the mayonnaise on each tortilla. Top with some of the pico de gallo, shredded cabbage, and avocado. Fold up the sides to form a taco.

Peanut Butter and Banana French Toast

DAIRY ■ YIELDS 4 SERVINGS

This sweet and creamy combination was popular at sandwich shops across the country in the 1950s.

8 slices soft white bread

¼ cup reduced-fat creamy or crunchy peanut butter

1 small banana, very thinly sliced

4 large eggs

3 tablespoons reduced-fat milk

⅛ teaspoon freshly ground black pepper

2 tablespoons butter

pancake syrup or honey, for serving

1. Arrange the bread on your work surface. Spread one tablespoon peanut butter on each of 4 slices. Top with banana slices. Cover with a second slice of bread.

2. Using the tines of a fork, press down around the outside of the bread to seal the 2 pieces together, enclosing the filling.

3. In a large bowl, whisk the eggs, milk, and pepper. Dip the sandwiches, one at a time, into the egg mixture, pressing down to saturate both sides. Turn the sandwiches over for a dunk on the second side if necessary. Don't let the bread sit in the mixture for long or it will get too soggy.

4. Melt the butter in a large nonstick skillet over medium heat. When the butter is melted and hot but not browned, add the sandwiches. Cook for 2 minutes per side, until golden but not brown. Flip each sandwich over and cook for 2 minutes on the second side until golden.

5. Transfer to plates and serve with pancake syrup or honey.

Spinach and Shells

DAIRY ■ YIELDS 6 SERVINGS

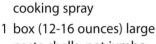

high heat or professional cooking spray

1 box (12-16 ounces) large pasta shells, not jumbo

water as needed

kosher salt or coarse sea salt

1 (10-ounce) box frozen spinach, defrosted for 2 minutes in microwave

2 cups (or 15-ounce container) part-skim ricotta cheese

2 cloves fresh garlic, minced

1 large egg

½ teaspoon fine sea salt

¼ teaspoon freshly ground black pepper

2 cups favorite jarred marinara sauce, divided

4 ounces shredded muenster or mozzarella cheese

You can also make this dish using rotini or fusilli pasta. Anything that will catch the spinach filling would work well.

1. Preheat oven to 350°F.

2. Spray a 10-inch round or square oven-to-table casserole dish with nonstick cooking spray.

3. Cook the pasta in a large pot of salted, rapidly boiling water according to the package instructions, until al dente. Drain and rinse under cold water to stop the cooking process.

4. Squeeze the water out of the spinach. Place spinach into a large mixing bowl. Add the ricotta cheese, garlic, egg, fine sea salt, and pepper. Mix well.

5. Add the cooked shells and stir.

6. Spread 1 cup marinara sauce in an even layer in the baking dish.

7. Pour the spinach and shells into the dish. Top with remaining sauce.

8. Sprinkle the shredded cheese evenly over the top.

9. Bake, uncovered, for 25–35 minutes or until cheese is melted, bubbly, and starting to brown. Serve hot.

Herbed Flounder Packages

PARVE ■ YIELDS 4 SERVINGS

1 cup loosely packed basil leaves

¼ cup fresh oregano leaves

⅛ teaspoon dried thyme

2 cloves fresh garlic, minced

1 teaspoon grated lemon zest

1 tablespoon lemon juice

¼ cup extra-virgin olive oil

4 (6-ounce) flounder fillets, skin and bones removed

fine sea salt

freshly ground black pepper

You will need a microplane to remove the zest from the lemon before squeezing it for the juice. If you don't have one, use a vegetable peeler to peel the thinnest layer of bright yellow lemon skin. Make sure not to get any white pith; it is bitter. Once you have removed the yellow zest, add it to the food processor or container.

1. Preheat oven to 400°F.

2. In a quart-sized container with an immersion blender or in the bowl of a food processor fitted with a metal "S" blade, pulse the basil leaves, oregano leaves, thyme, garlic, lemon zest, lemon juice, and olive oil until chopped. Don't grind too finely. Set aside.

3. Place each fish fillet into the center of a piece of aluminum foil large enough to fully enclose it. Season each fillet with salt and pepper.

4. Divide the herb mixture evenly and smear over the top of each fillet. Bring up the sides of the foil to enclose the packages and place them on a foil-lined jelly roll pan.

5. Bake for 5–7 minutes, until the fish flakes easily from the thickest part when tested with a fork.

6. Transfer packets to plates and serve hot.

Pasta Quattro Formaggio

DAIRY ■ YIELDS 10 SERVINGS

1 pound penne pasta

water as needed

kosher salt or coarse sea salt

2½ cups milk

1 cup mascarpone cheese

2 tablespoons all-purpose flour

⅛ teaspoon ground nutmeg

½ cup grated Romano cheese

½ cup grated Parmesan cheese

⅛ teaspoon ground white pepper

⅛ teaspoon fine sea salt

1 cup shredded mozzarella

This means "pasta with 4 cheeses" in Italian and it is an absolutely incredible, creamy, rich sauce. For a tangier sauce, you can substitute blue cheese crumbles for the mascarpone, which is a sweet Italian cheese available kosher in most regular supermarkets. It is creamy and comes in a tub.

This dish needs to be eaten as soon as the sauce hits the pasta. If you are cooking in advance, cook your pasta until al dente, rinse with very cold water to stop the cooking, and toss it with a little olive oil. Before serving, bring a pot of water to a boil, dunk the pasta for 5 seconds and drain. To make the sauce in advance, cook it completely then allow to cool. When ready to use, heat 2 tablespoons water in a pot on very low heat. Add the sauce and whisk over the low heat until warm, making sure the bottom does not scorch.

1. Cook the pasta in a large pot of salted, rapidly boiling water according to the package instructions, until al dente. Drain and rinse under cold water to stop the cooking process. Transfer to large serving bowl.

2. Meanwhile, pour the milk, mascarpone, flour, and nutmeg into a medium pot. Whisking the whole time for 8 minutes, cook over medium heat until thick enough to coat a wooden spoon. To test, stir the sauce with a wooden spoon and lift the spoon out of the sauce. Drag your finger down the center of the spoon; the line will remain if the sauce is thick enough.

3. Add the Romano and Parmesan cheeses. Whisk for another 2 minutes. Add the white pepper, salt, and mozzarella. Whisk until the sauce is smooth and the cheeses are melted. Pour over the pasta; toss to coat.

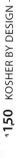

(V)
(NF)
(DF)

Vegan

Portobello Burgers

PARVE ■ YIELDS 6 SERVINGS

6 (3-inch diameter) Portobello mushroom caps, brushed clean

1-2 medium red onions, peeled, cut into ½-inch-thick slices (keep rings together)

⅔ cup olive oil

¼ cup balsamic vinegar

6 cloves fresh garlic, minced

½ teaspoon dried thyme, crumbled

½ teaspoon dried oregano leaves

1 teaspoon coarse sea salt

½ teaspoon freshly ground black pepper

high heat or professional cooking spray

6 ciabatta rolls or kaiser rolls

honey mustard (I like Honeycup® brand) or low-fat mayonnaise

1 beefsteak tomato, thinly sliced

1 avocado, pitted and peeled, cut into slices

This recipe was written parve, but feel free to melt any kind of cheese — from crumbled feta, blue cheese, mozzarella, to Monterey Jack — over the mushroom caps.

1. Snap the stems from each mushroom cap. Reserve stems for another use or discard. Using a spoon, scrape out the gills from the mushroom cap and discard. Place caps into a shallow container in a single layer along with the onion slices.

2. In a medium bowl, whisk the olive oil, balsamic vinegar, garlic, thyme, oregano, salt, and pepper. Pour over the mushrooms and marinate for 15 minutes.

3. Spray a grill pan or skillet with nonstick cooking spray. Heat over medium until very hot but not smoking. Remove mushrooms and onions from marinade; reserve marinade. Add the mushrooms and onions to the grill pan. Cook for 4 minutes, until the mushrooms and onions start to soften. Use tongs to flip and cook on the second side for an additional 4–5 minutes. Remove the mushrooms and onions.

4. Cut rolls in half. Brush with reserved marinade. Place the rolls cut side down in the pan; toast, allowing the bread to soak up the flavors, about 2–3 minutes.

5. Spread honey mustard or mayonnaise on half of the roll.

6. Place the mushroom on the other half of the roll; top with a slice or two of onion, tomato, and avocado. Cover with top of the roll. Eat the sandwich hot.

Broccoli Quiche

DAIRY ■ YIELDS 8 SERVINGS

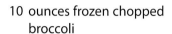

10 ounces frozen chopped broccoli

1 (9-inch) frozen deep-dish pie crust

3 ounces sliced Swiss cheese, stacked and cut into small squares

¾ cup heavy cream

¾ cup milk

1 large egg plus 2 egg yolks

1 teaspoon fine sea salt

¼ teaspoon ground white pepper

I always liked quiche but after tasting Chef Damian Sansonetti's version I fell in love. A green salad on the side and you have an awesome brunch, lunch, or dinner. I've even been known to eat a slice right out of the fridge for a late-night snack.

1. Place the frozen broccoli into a strainer. Run it under hot water and drain, allowing the broccoli to defrost.

2. Preheat oven to 350°F. Place the pie shell on a cookie sheet, prick with a fork, and bake for 15 minutes until light golden brown. Remove from oven. Gently press the bottom of the crust down if it has bubbled up. Cool. Raise the oven temperature to 375°F.

3. Place drained broccoli and cheese squares into a bowl. Toss with your hands to distribute the cheese into the broccoli. Pour into the baked crust.

4. In a medium bowl, whisk the heavy cream, milk, egg, egg yolks, salt, and white pepper. Pour the egg mixture over the broccoli. Use the back of a spoon to press the broccoli down and spread the liquid. If not using a deep-dish crust, you will have too much filling; make sure it doesn't overflow.

5. Place the quiche, on its cookie sheet to catch any spills, into the oven. Bake 45 minutes or until a toothpick or the tip of a small sharp knife inserted into the center comes out clean.

6. Serve hot or at room temperature.

New Tuna-Noodle Casserole

DAIRY ■ YIELDS 8-10 SERVINGS

ⓃⒻ

high heat or professional cooking spray

1 (12-ounce) bag extra-broad egg noodles (yolk-free noodles, if possible)

kosher salt or coarse sea salt

water as needed

1 (12-ounce) can white albacore tuna, packed in water, drained

1 cup frozen peas

1 tablespoon olive oil

½ medium onion, peeled, cut into ¼-inch dice

8 ounces button or crimini mushrooms, brushed clean and sliced

2 tablespoons unsalted butter

2 tablespoons all-purpose flour

1 cup low-fat milk

¼ teaspoon fine sea salt

8 ounces shredded cheddar cheese

½ cup cornflake crumbs or breadcrumbs

1 tablespoon butter, melted

When I was a kid, my mom used to make a tuna-noodle casserole that my sister and I loved. But I do remember that I always picked out the canned peas, which would get all smooshed and yucky, and try to toss them before my mom saw. The recipe had a lot of processed ingredients and canned items, so I took a crack at updating it and it is fresher, healthier, and fabulous in its new incarnation! I like using the "No Yolks"® noodles; in this recipe the cholesterol from egg yolks is not missed. I watched my kids eat it, and not a pretty green pea was left over!

This recipe feeds a crowd but can easily be halved for just 4 or 5 eaters.

1. Preheat oven to 350°F.

2. Spray a 9-by-13-inch baking dish with nonstick cooking spray.

3. Cook the pasta in a large pot of salted, rapidly boiling water according to the package instructions, until al dente. Drain and rinse under cold water to stop the cooking process. Transfer to the prepared baking dish. Add the drained tuna, using a fork or your fingers to break it up and distribute through the noodles. Add the peas. Set aside.

4. Meanwhile, in a medium pot, heat the olive oil. Add the onion and mushrooms. Sauté until soft and fragrant, 5–6 minutes, stirring with a wooden spoon. Add the 2 tablespoons butter and stir to melt it and distribute it through the onions. Sprinkle on the flour. Stir until mixture becomes sticky. Slowly pour in the milk, stirring to make a smooth sauce. Add the salt. Stir in the cheese. As it melts, the sauce will thicken. Pour over the noodles and mix well.

5. In a small bowl, mix the cornflake crumbs with the melted butter. Sprinkle over the top of the noodles. Bake, uncovered, for 15 minutes or until heated through. Serve hot.

Pita Pizzas

DAIRY OR PARVE ■ YIELDS 6 SERVINGS

In my early teens, my girlfriend Shari Wiesel and I spent almost every Saturday night together. We even babysat as a tag-team, two for the price of one! We would inevitably end up back at one of our houses whipping up pita pizzas as a late-night snack.

We always went traditional, but there is an unlimited number of ingredients that can be baked on a pita for a quick snack or meal. Here are some ideas to get you started.

The mushroom-olive and pesto pizzas are cheeseless, so are also nice at a meat or parve meal. There are no amounts for sauces, spices, or cheese; this is a personal choice. Just don't overload a pita!

TRADITIONAL PIZZA:

- 6 plain or whole-wheat pita breads
- marinara sauce
- mozzarella cheese
- dried oregano leaves
- crushed red pepper flakes
- freshly ground black pepper

TRADITIONAL PIZZA:

1. Preheat oven to 425°F. Place the pita breads on a cookie sheet.
2. Using a spoon, spread each pita with marinara sauce. Sprinkle the cheese on the sauce. Season with oregano, red pepper flakes, and black pepper.
3. Bake for 8-10 minutes, until the cheese is melted and bubbly. Serve hot.

PESTO PIZZA:

- 6 plain or whole-wheat pita breads
- olive oil
- prepared pesto
- 2-3 firm plum tomatoes, thinly sliced
- 1 jarred roasted red pepper, rinsed, drained, and sliced into strips

PESTO PIZZA:

1. Preheat oven to 425°F. Place the pita breads on a cookie sheet. Lightly brush each with olive oil.
2. Using a spoon, spread each pita with pesto. Arrange tomato slices and red pepper strips on the pesto.
3. Bake for 8-10 minutes. Serve hot.

more pizza on next page

MUSHROOM-ONION-GOAT CHEESE PIZZA:

6 plain or whole-wheat pita breads

olive oil

2 large red onions, peeled, sliced into thin rings

pinch of sugar

¼ teaspoon fine sea salt

4 cloves fresh garlic, sliced

12 crimini mushrooms, brushed clean and sliced

1 tablespoon balsamic vinegar

4-5 ounces goat cheese crumbles

MUSHROOM-ONION-GOAT CHEESE PIZZA:

1. Preheat oven to 425°F. Place the pita breads on a cookie sheet. Lightly brush with olive oil. Set aside.

2. Heat one tablespoon olive oil in a large pot. Add the onion, sugar, and salt. Slowly cook and stir over medium heat for 15 minutes, until the onions are soft and caramelized. Add the garlic and mushrooms and cook for another 5 minutes. Add the balsamic. Stir and cook for 5 minutes longer.

3. Spread on pita breads. Top with goat cheese crumbles.

4. Bake for 8-10 minutes. Serve hot.

RICOTTA-SPINACH PIZZA:

6 plain or whole-wheat pita breads

ricotta cheese

frozen chopped spinach, defrosted and squeezed dry

ground white pepper

garlic powder

2-3 firm plum tomatoes, thinly sliced

RICOTTA-SPINACH PIZZA:

1. Preheat oven to 425°F. Place the pita breads on a cookie sheet.

2. Using a spoon, spread each pita with ricotta cheese. Sprinkle on the spinach. Season with white pepper and garlic powder. Top with tomato slices.

3. Bake for 8-10 minutes. Serve hot.

MUSHROOM-OLIVE PIZZA:

6 plain or whole-wheat pita breads

favorite jarred marinara sauce

5-6 white button mushrooms, brushed clean and sliced

canned sliced black olives, drained

dried oregano leaves

freshly ground black pepper

MUSHROOM-OLIVE PIZZA:

1. Preheat oven to 425°F. Place the pita breads on a cookie sheet.

2. Using a spoon, spread each pita with marinara sauce. Sprinkle on the mushrooms and olives.

3. Season with oregano and black pepper.

4. Bake for 8-10 minutes. Serve hot.

Side Dishes

Confetti Spaghetti Squash

DAIRY ■ YIELDS 4-6 SERVINGS

1 medium spaghetti squash, about 2½-3 pounds

2 tablespoons olive oil

2 tablespoons pine nuts

1 small red onion, peeled, thinly sliced

1 teaspoon dried oregano leaves

4 cloves fresh garlic, very thinly sliced

1 cup halved grape tomatoes

¼ cup sliced black olives, from a small can, drained

½ teaspoon fine sea salt

½ teaspoon freshly ground black pepper

4 ounces goat cheese or feta cheese, crumbled

Spaghetti squash is a fabulous vegetable. Granted, my teens don't think it passes as pasta even if the strands of squash do look like spaghetti. Regardless, they think it looks cool, tastes great, and is so good for you. You can season the strands any way you want, from simply melting in some butter and garlic to a marinara sauce topping. I have even used leftovers by pressing them into patties, breading in breadcrumbs, and pan-searing for a great squash patty.

1. Preheat oven to 400°F.

2. Place the whole spaghetti squash on a parchment-lined jelly roll pan. Roast, uncovered, for 55–60 minutes. It is done when you can easily pierce it with a fork. Remove the pan from the oven and set the squash aside to cool for a few minutes so it is easier to handle.

3. Meanwhile, heat the olive oil in a large skillet over medium heat. Add the pine nuts and toast until they are fragrant. Add the red onion and oregano and cook until soft and shiny. Add the garlic and cook for another 3 minutes, until garlic is fragrant. Don't allow the garlic or onions to brown. Add the tomatoes and olives. Heat through. Turn off the heat.

4. Cut the squash in half lengthwise. Using a large spoon, remove and discard the seeds. Using a large fork, drag the flesh of the squash from top to bottom, away from the skin. The strands will look like spaghetti. Turn the heat back on under the skillet. Add the strands of spaghetti squash. Toss to mix all the ingredients. Season with salt and pepper. Add the cheese crumbles and cook until heated through.

5. Transfer to a serving bowl or individual plates.

Maple-Roasted
Pears and Sweet Potatoes

DAIRY OR PARVE ■ YIELDS 6 SERVINGS

8 mini pears, such as Seckel, or 4 ripe Anjou pears, peeled, halved, cored, quartered

3 large sweet potatoes (about 2 pounds), peeled, halved lengthwise, and cut into chunks the same size as the pears

6 tablespoons butter or margarine

1 cup pure maple syrup (NOT pancake syrup)

½ teaspoon coarse sea salt or kosher salt

I adore these soft sweet pears and the way the sweet potatoes become sticky and sweet. You can try this with cubed butternut squash in addition to or in place of the sweet potatoes. While you have the maple syrup on hand, put the Pineapple Maple Glazed Salmon (page 134) on your menu for another night.

1. Preheat oven to 325°F.

2. For easy cleanup, completely cover a small jelly roll pan with aluminum foil. Set aside.

3. As you cut up the pears and sweet potatoes, place them into a large bowl. Set aside.

4. In a medium pot, melt the butter or margarine over medium heat. Whisk in maple syrup and salt. Cook until it starts to bubble.

5. Remove from heat. Pour over the pears and sweet potatoes. Toss to coat. Transfer to prepared pan.

6. Bake, uncovered, for 1½ hours.

7. Transfer to a serving bowl or platter.

delish

Za'atar Cauliflower

MEAT OR PARVE ■ YIELDS 4 SERVINGS

1 head cauliflower

2 tablespoons olive oil

2 tablespoons za'atar seasoning

2 tablespoons chicken or vegetable broth

4 cloves fresh garlic, minced

This recipe is easily doubled — and I recommend it. These are awesome to snack on right out of the oven, so they don't always make it to the table.

1. Place an empty jelly roll pan into the oven. Turn the oven to 450°F, allowing the pan to heat as the oven does. This will help crisp the cauliflower as it begins to roast.

2. Turn the head of cauliflower stem side up. Using a knife, cut the head in half. Cut the cauliflower off the core into small florets. Discard the core and leaves.

3. In a very large bowl, whisk the olive oil, za'atar, broth, and minced garlic. Add the cauliflower, including the tiniest florets that broke off. Use both hands to really toss until all the cauliflower is evenly coated with the spice mixture.

4. Carefully remove the hot pan from the oven. Pour the cauliflower in a single, even layer into the pan. Using oven mitts, since the pan will be hot, return the pan to the oven and roast, uncovered, for 30–40 minutes, depending on the size of the florets.

Toasted Sesame Rice

PARVE ■ YIELDS 6 SERVINGS

2 cups white basmati rice

3¼ cups water

¼ cup roasted or toasted sesame oil

1 teaspoon sesame seeds

1 teaspoon black sesame seeds

2 scallions, roots trimmed and discarded, very thinly sliced on the diagonal

½ teaspoon fine sea salt

¼ teaspoon freshly ground black pepper

This rice may look plain, but the subtle sesame flavor makes it the perfect accompaniment for almost any chicken, fish, or meat dish.

1. Place the rice and water into a medium pot. Bring to a boil, uncovered, over medium heat. Cook for 5 minutes. Place the cover on the pot and turn off the heat. Allow the rice to steam in the covered pot for 15 minutes.

2. Remove the cover. Stir in the sesame oil, sesame seeds, black sesame seeds, scallions, salt, and pepper. Toss.

3. Transfer to serving bowl.

Bamboo
Chopsticks

福壽康寧

Barbecued Potato Kugel

PARVE ■ YIELDS 9 SERVINGS

2 large eggs
1 tablespoon smoked paprika
2 teaspoons light brown sugar
2 teaspoons fine sea salt
1 teaspoon baking powder
½ teaspoon finely ground black pepper
¼ teaspoon onion powder
2½ pounds Yukon Gold potatoes
1 medium onion, peeled and cut into thirds
⅓ cup canola oil

This is an awesome take on a classic! The smoked paprika is the spice used on barbecue potato chips and adds the same smoky flavor to this winner. As with all potato kugels, it is best served within 2 hours of baking to retain its moist and fluffy inside and crisp top.

When selecting your baking dish, refrain from using a Pyrex dish. The extreme changes in temperature can cause it to explode, a very messy and dangerous situation.

1. Place a 9-by-9-inch baking pan, oven-to-table casserole, or baking dish into the oven. Turn the oven on and set to 375°F, allowing the pan to heat as the oven comes to temperature.

2. In a medium bowl, whisk the eggs, smoked paprika, brown sugar, salt, baking powder, pepper, and onion powder. Make sure the eggs are well beaten and a little bubbly. Set aside.

3. Peel all the potatoes. Cut each into quarters. Take one-third of the potatoes and one-third of the onion and place into a food processor fitted with a metal "S" blade. Purée until smooth. Using a silicone spatula, empty the bowl of the food processor into a large bowl. Repeat this 2 more times until all the potatoes and onion have been puréed.

4. Add the egg mixture into the potatoes and mix well.

5. Carefully remove the baking dish from the oven; remember, the pan will be very hot. Facing the pan away from you, to keep the oil from splattering you, pour the oil into the pan. Carefully transfer the potatoes into the pan. Use a spoon to scoop up some of the oil that comes up from the sides and drizzle it all over the potatoes.

6. Bake, uncovered, for 1 hour 30 minutes. Serve hot and within 2 hours of baking.

Creamy Parsnips-Spinach

DAIRY OR PARVE ■ YIELDS 8 SERVINGS

1 tablespoon olive oil

½ medium onion, peeled, cut into ¼-inch dice

4 cloves fresh garlic, thinly sliced

4 medium parsnips, peeled, cut into ¼-inch rounds

2 cups light cream or unsweetened plain soy milk

1 cup water

2 (10-ounce) boxes frozen chopped spinach, defrosted for 20 minutes

½ teaspoon onion powder

½ teaspoon garlic powder

½ teaspoon fine sea salt

¼ teaspoon freshly ground black pepper

tiny pinch of nutmeg (less than ⅛ teaspoon)

My daughter Kate loves parsnips and creamed spinach, so I developed this recipe as a mixture of both. Parsnips look like a white version of carrots but have a much sweeter flavor that becomes intensified when cooked. If you are making this dish in advance, when reheating you may need to add a little milk, soy milk, or stock, since it thickens as it cools.

1. Heat the olive oil in a large pot over medium heat. Add the onion and sauté for 4–5 minutes until translucent; do not brown, just become golden.

2. Sprinkle in the garlic and sauté for 3 minutes, until the garlic is fragrant.

3. Add the parsnips and cream or soy milk. Simmer for 15 minutes; it will get bubbly.

4. Add the water; heat through. Turn off the heat. Use an immersion blender right in the pot to blend until smooth.

5. Return to a medium heat. Break the partially defrosted spinach into chunks and add them to the pot. Chop and stir with a wooden spoon. Season with onion powder, garlic powder, salt, pepper, and nutmeg. Stir well and heat through.

6. Transfer to a serving bowl. Serve hot.

Hoisin Vegetables

PARVE ■ YIELDS 4 SERVINGS

olive oil

2 Asian eggplants, with skin, sliced into ¼-inch rounds

3 medium (3-inch diameter) portobello mushroom caps, gills scooped out and discarded, sliced into ½-inch slices

2 tablespoons hoisin sauce

1 tablespoon soy sauce

juice of ½ lemon

1 tablespoon honey

1 teaspoon rice vinegar

½ teaspoon garlic powder

¼ teaspoon fine sea salt

¼ teaspoon freshly ground black pepper

Feel free to add any vegetables that you have in the bin. I've tossed in broccoli florets, cauliflower, red pepper strips — even carrots.

1. Pour olive oil to a depth of ¼-inch into a very large skillet. The amount will depend on the size of your skillet. Heat the oil over medium heat until very hot but not smoking.

2. Add the eggplant and mushrooms. Sauté until the eggplant starts to turn golden, flipping the pieces to sauté the second side of all the vegetables.

3. In a small bowl, whisk the hoisin, soy sauce, lemon juice, honey, vinegar, garlic powder, salt, and pepper until smooth. Add to the skillet. Sauté while stirring to coat all the vegetables. Cook until they are slightly limp.

4. Remove to a platter and serve warm.

(V) (NF) (DF) (GF)

Spicy Carrot Sticks

PARVE ■ YIELDS 4-6 SERVINGS

6 large carrots, peeled, ends trimmed

1 egg white from a large egg

3 tablespoons olive oil

1 tablespoon water

1½ teaspoons garlic powder

1½ teaspoons ground cumin

1½ teaspoons sugar

½ teaspoon paprika

¼ teaspoon ground white pepper

1 teaspoon coarse sea salt or kosher salt

I have always been a fan of roasting any vegetable at a high heat to caramelize its natural sugars. This fantastic side dish goes a step further by adding a spicy kick that makes these carrots addictive.

1. Preheat oven to 450°F. Line a jelly roll pan with parchment paper. Set aside.

2. Cut each carrot in half to make 2 (3–4 inch) pieces.

3. Cut each carrot half in half lengthwise. With the cut-side-down on your cutting board, cut each half into 3 equal strips to make carrot sticks.

4. Place the egg white into a large shallow bowl or container and whip with a fork or whisk till foamy.

5. In a large bowl, mix the olive oil, water, garlic powder, cumin, sugar, paprika, and white pepper.

6. Place the carrot sticks into the beaten egg; turning to coat the carrots in the egg white.

7. Remove the carrots from the egg white and stir into the spice mixture. Arrange in a single layer on the prepared pan. Sprinkle with salt.

8. Roast, uncovered, for 20 minutes.

9. Transfer to a serving plate or bowl.

Parmesan Quinoa

1 cup quinoa

2 cups water

1 tablespoon butter

¼ teaspoon fine sea salt

½ cup grated Parmesan cheese

My very own teen-in-the-kitchen, Danielle, created this dish for a dairy Passover meal. We loved it so much we started making it all year 'round. I hope you'll make this recipe because it is so delicious but also know what a great favor you are doing your body by eating it. Quinoa is a seed, not a grain. Our bodies cannot create amino acids, we must get them from food — so it's important to consume them whenever possible, and quinoa contains all essential amino acids. Few meatless proteins contain all amino acids, so if you are vegetarian, quinoa is a great way to provide yourself with a well-rounded protein. It's a good source of fiber, iron, vitamins, and minerals. It even packs in some healthy fats in the form of Omega-3 fatty acids. No wonder this powerhouse superfood is catching on so quickly!

1. Rinse the quinoa by placing it in a medium bowl, covering with water, swishing it around, and then draining it in a strainer. This will wash away any naturally occurring bitterness from the quinoa.

2. Place the drained quinoa into a medium pot. Add the 2 cups water, butter, and salt. Bring to a boil. Lower to a simmer and allow the quinoa to bubble and cook for 15 minutes until the quinoa absorbs all the liquid. The outer germ layer will separate and the grains will look shiny.

3. Stir in the Parmesan. Serve warm or at room temperature.

Banana-Pumpkin Cornbread

DAIRY OR PARVE ■ YIELDS 10 SERVINGS

high heat or professional
  cooking spray
1½ cups all-purpose flour
 ¾ cup finely ground
    cornmeal (NOT cornstarch)
 2 teaspoons baking powder
 ½ teaspoon fine sea salt
 ½ cup (1 stick) butter or
    margarine, softened
    for 15 minutes at room
    temperature
 ½ cup sugar
 ¾ cup dark brown sugar
 3 large eggs
1½ cups (2-4 medium) ripe
    bananas, peeled and
    mashed
 ¾ cup canned pure pumpkin
    purée (NOT pumpkin pie
    filling)

This versatile recipe makes a wonderful side dish but also keep it in mind for serving with soup or a salad. You can even toast a slice and serve with a smear of butter for breakfast.

1. Preheat oven to 350°F. Spray a 9-by-5-inch loaf pan with nonstick cooking spray.

2. In a medium bowl, whisk the flour, cornmeal, baking powder, and salt. Set aside.

3. In the bowl of a stand mixer, beat the butter or margarine with the sugar and brown sugar until fluffy and creamy. Add the eggs, one at a time, mixing until incorporated. Add the bananas and pumpkin. Beat until smooth. Slowly mix in the flour mixture just until combined; do not overbeat.

4. Scoop the batter into the prepared loaf pan. Bake for 1 hour 10 minutes. When you insert a toothpick into the center of the loaf, it should come out clean. Let the bread cool in the pan for 10 minutes. Remove from pan and serve warm or cool completely on a wire rack.

Smashed Potatoes

PARVE ■ YIELDS 4 SERVINGS

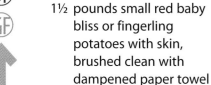

1½ pounds small red baby bliss or fingerling potatoes with skin, brushed clean with dampened paper towel

water to cover

1 tablespoon plus 1 teaspoon kosher salt, divided

½ teaspoon coarsely ground black pepper

½ teaspoon crushed dried rosemary

½ cup olive oil, divided

8 cloves fresh garlic, thinly sliced

You can buy dried rosemary already crushed, but if yours isn't, put 1 teaspoon regular dried rosemary on a cutting board and chop finely with your knife.

1. Cut larger potatoes in half. Place the potatoes into a large pot. Add just enough water to cover. Add 1 tablespoon kosher salt.

2. Bring to a boil and cook for 20 minutes or until the largest potatoes are easily pierced with a fork.

3. Meanwhile, in a small bowl, combine ½ teaspoon kosher salt, pepper, and rosemary. Set aside.

4. Pour the potatoes into a colander and drain. Place on a jelly roll pan.

5. Return the empty pot to the stove. Add half the oil (¼ cup) and the sliced garlic and heat over medium. Cook until the garlic is golden, about 15 seconds, making sure the garlic does not brown. Remove it with a slotted spoon or spatula and set aside.

6. Using the bottom of a measuring cup or your palm, smash each potato — be careful, they will be hot. Carefully place half the potatoes into the pot in a single layer. Cook the smashed potatoes until they start to become golden, 3–4 minutes. Flip with a metal spatula, scraping the bottom of the pot, and cook until golden on the second side, 3–4 minutes. Return to the jelly roll pan. Heat remaining oil. Cook the second batch of potatoes.

7. Place the finished potatoes on a platter. Sprinkle on the rosemary mixture and garlic.

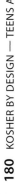

Szechuan Noodles

PARVE ■ YIELDS 6-8 SERVINGS

1 (16-ounce) box linguini pasta

water as needed

kosher salt

½ cup reduced-fat peanut butter

¼ cup soy sauce

¼ cup water

2 tablespoons rice vinegar

2 tablespoons roasted or toasted sesame oil

1 tablespoon teriyaki sauce

1 tablespoon honey

2 cloves fresh garlic, minced

¼ teaspoon fine sea salt

⅛ teaspoon ground ginger

1 tablespoon canola or olive oil

15 snow peas, each sliced in half lengthwise

5 shiitake mushrooms, brushed clean, stems discarded, sliced

1 red bell pepper, seeded, sliced into very thin (⅛-inch) strips

¼ cup shredded carrots

2 scallions, roots trimmed and discarded, thinly sliced

You can turn this into a main dish by adding grilled chicken or, for vegetarians, grilled tempeh.

1. Cook the pasta in a large pot of salted, rapidly boiling water according to the package instructions, until al dente. Drain and rinse under cold water to stop the cooking process.

2. In a small pot, whisk the peanut butter, soy sauce, ¼ cup water, vinegar, sesame oil, teriyaki sauce, honey, garlic, salt, and ginger. Heat over medium and whisk until smooth and warm.

3. Heat the oil in a large skillet over medium heat. Sauté the snow peas, shiitakes, red pepper, carrots, and scallions for 5–6 minutes until shiny and slightly limp.

4. In large bowl, toss the linguini with the peanut sauce and vegetables. Serve hot or at room temperature. If served at room temperature, the sauce will thicken.

Asian Green Beans

PARVE ■ YIELDS 4-6 SERVINGS

¾ pound green beans,
  trimmed, or haricots verts

water as needed

2 tablespoons soy sauce

2 tablespoons maple syrup
  (NOT pancake syrup)

2 cloves fresh garlic,
  minced

¼ teaspoon ground ginger

This classic combo of green beans paired with Asian flavors will leave you licking your fingers.

1. Place the green beans into a medium pot. Cover with water. Bring to a boil and simmer for 4–5 minutes, until the green beans turn a bright green. Drain. Return the green beans to the pot and set aside.

2. In a small bowl, whisk the soy sauce, maple syrup, garlic, and ginger. Pour the soy mixture over the green beans. Over medium heat, warm the sauce and toss the green beans to coat.

3. Transfer to a serving bowl.

Desserts

Chocolate Tart in Pretzel Crust

DAIRY ■ YIELDS 10-12 SERVINGS

CRUST:
- 6 chocolate sandwich cookies, such as Oreos®
- 2 cups mini salted pretzel twists
- 6 tablespoons butter, melted

CHOCOLATE FILLING:
- 1 (4-ounce) good-quality semisweet chocolate bars, such as Ghiradelli®
- 1 (4-ounce) good-quality milk chocolate bar, such as Ghiradelli®
- 1 cup heavy cream
- whipped cream, optional for garnish
- additional mini salted pretzel twists for optional garnish

Measure the pretzels by stacking them in a 1-cup measuring cup, using slight pressure from your palm to fill the cup.

1. Preheat oven to 350°F.

2. Place the pretzels and cookies into the bowl of a food processor fitted with a metal "S" blade. Pulse until almost fine; some small pretzel pieces should remain. Pour into mixing bowl. Add the melted butter. Stir to moisten the crumbs. Transfer into a 9-inch glass pie plate or a 9-inch tart pan with removable bottom. Use the bottom of a measuring cup or your palm to press mixture into an even layer on the bottom and up the sides of the pan. Place the pan on a cookie sheet for easy transfer to and from the oven. Bake for 15 minutes. Set aside to cool.

3. Place the chocolate on your cutting board. Using a sharp knife, finely chop the chocolate.

4. Heat the cream in a medium pot until it is simmering. Add the chocolate, including any small shards from the cutting board. Turn off the heat. Stir until smooth and chocolatey throughout. Pour into the prepared crust and chill for at least 2 hours.

5. Slice and serve plain or with whipped cream and pretzels.

Honey Cookies

PARVE ■ YIELDS 20-22 COOKIES

2¾ cups all-purpose flour

2 teaspoons baking powder

1 teaspoon ground cinnamon

½ teaspoon ground ginger

½ teaspoon fine sea salt

1 large egg

1 cup sugar

¾ cup canola oil

½ cup honey

1 teaspoon pure vanilla extract

turbinado, also known as raw sugar, or demerara sugar, for rolling

Coating the dough balls in turbinado or demerara sugar gives these chewy cookies a nice crunch. Unlike typical granulated sugar, turbinado sugar crystals are much larger, and are made at an earlier period in the sugar cane processing method. They retain some of the flavor of molasses, a natural byproduct of the sugar process, so they also give a deeper brown-sugary flavor. If you don't have it, you can roll the balls in regular sugar, but they will be a little more pale and they will lack the crunch.

1. Preheat oven to 350°F. Line two cookie sheets with parchment paper. Set aside.

2. In a medium bowl, whisk the flour, baking powder, cinnamon, ginger, and salt. Set aside.

3. In the bowl of a stand mixer set to medium speed, beat the egg and sugar until creamy and light.

4. Turn down the speed and add the canola oil. Return to medium speed and beat.

5. Measure the honey in the cup used for the oil; this will help the honey slide right out. Add to the bowl. Add the vanilla. Mix.

6. Stir in the flour mixture.

7. Pour ½ cup turbinado or demerara sugar into a small bowl.

8. Using a small ice-cream scooper or by pinching a ball with your fingers, scoop out walnut-sized balls of dough. Roll between your palms to form small balls. Roll the dough balls in the sugar to coat. Place onto the prepared cookie sheets. Bake for 11–12 minutes until golden and flattened.

9. Remove from sheets and allow to cool for 5 minutes. Transfer the cookies to a rack to cool completely.

Peach-Apricot Cobbler

DAIRY OR PARVE ■ YIELDS 10 SERVINGS

- 4 apricots
- 5 peaches, peeled
- ⅓ cup sugar
- ¾ teaspoon ground cinnamon
- ¼ teaspoon fine sea salt
- 1 tablespoon cornstarch
- ½ cup all-purpose flour
- ½ cup sugar
- ¾ teaspoon baking powder
- ¼ teaspoon fine sea salt
- 1 large egg, lightly beaten in a bowl with a fork till foamy
- 2 tablespoons butter or margarine, melted in microwave for 30 seconds
- ⅓ cup sugar mixed with 1 tablespoon ground cinnamon

This is a perfect summer dessert. In early Fall, peaches go out of season but there is no reason to shelve this dessert. You can substitute 2½ pounds quick-frozen peach slices, and they are already peeled and sliced, which makes them easy to use. Defrost them before starting the recipe, drain liquid if needed, and then pat them dry with paper towels. If necessary, you can defrost the peaches in the microwave; it will take 4–5 minutes on high. For the apricots, it is hard to find quick-frozen ones, so just use apricots from a can. Count out 8 halves and make sure they are drained. This version will be more liquidy, so use twice the amount of cornstarch; otherwise, follow the recipe as written.

1. Cut each apricot down the middle; separate the halves. Remove the pit and discard it. Cut each half into 4 strips, lengthwise. Do the same thing with the peeled peaches. Place the apricot and peach slices into a large bowl. Toss with ⅓ cup sugar, ¾ teaspoon cinnamon, ¼ teaspoon salt, and cornstarch. Once fruit is mixed well, allow it to stand for 20 minutes.

2. Preheat oven to 400°F.

3. Transfer the mixture to a pretty oven-to-table casserole or Pyrex baking dish that it will fit snugly. It can be any shape, but as a guide you can use a 9-by-9-inch square. For easy cleanup, place the pan on a foil-lined cookie sheet. Bake for 35–40 minutes, until bubbly around the edges.

4. In a medium bowl, whisk the flour, ½ cup sugar, baking powder, and ¼ teaspoon salt. Make a well in the center of the bowl, pushing the flour mixture to the sides. Drop in the egg and the melted butter or margarine. Stir until a smooth batter forms.

5. Carefully remove baking dish from oven. Dollop the batter over the fruit, starting at the center, leaving a border that will not be covered. Using a knife or thin spatula, very gently spread the batter into a thin layer over the fruit. Sprinkle the cinnamon/sugar evenly over the whole cobbler.

6. Return the dish to the oven and bake, uncovered, for 30 minutes.

7. Allow the cobbler to rest for 10 minutes before serving. This is great served with peach or vanilla ice cream.

Tie-Dye Cookies

DAIRY OR PARVE ■ YIELDS 30-32 COOKIES

1¼ cups all-purpose flour

1 teaspoon cream of tartar

½ teaspoon baking soda

½ teaspoon fine sea salt

½ cup (1 stick) butter or margarine, at room temperature for 15 minutes

¾ cup sugar

1 large egg

½ teaspoon pure vanilla extract

3 different food colorings; gels work best

Hip, colorful, and fun. Just make sure you wear disposable gloves so your hands aren't colorful and fun for hours after you've baked these yummy cookies.

1. Preheat oven to 400°F.

2. Line 2 cookie sheets with parchment paper. Set aside.

3. In a medium bowl, whisk the flour, cream of tartar, baking soda, and salt. Set aside.

4. In the bowl of a stand mixer, cream the butter or margarine and sugar on high until pale yellow and fluffy. Add the egg and vanilla. Beat until combined. Add the flour mixture, a scoop at a time, mixing after you add each scoop.

5. Divide the dough into 3 equal pieces. Leave one piece in the mixing bowl, and place the other two pieces on paper plates or sheets of parchment paper.

6. If the food coloring is a liquid, add 6–7 drops of one of the colors to the bowl. If it is a gel, add ¼ teaspoon of the gel to the dough in the mixing bowl. Turn the mixer on and beat until the color is evenly distributed. You can do this by hand as well. Wearing disposable gloves to keep the color off your skin, and working on a piece of parchment paper to keep it off your countertop, knead the coloring into the dough until it is uniform. Repeat with the other two colors and pieces of dough until you have 3 pieces of colored dough. If the dough is too soft to work with, place into the refrigerator for about 30 minutes to firm up.

7. Rip off ½ teaspoon of each of the 3 colored doughs and roll them together, kneading the colors a little bit so you get a tie-dyed effect. Roll into a ball. Place onto the prepared cookie sheet. Leave room; they will spread. Repeat until all the dough is used.

8. Bake for 10 minutes. If baking two trays at the same time, switch the trays halfway through the baking time.

9. Remove the cookies from the sheet with a spatula and place them on a rack to cool completely.

Chocolate Chocolate Chip Sticks

DAIRY OR PARVE ■ YIELDS 24-26 COOKIE STICKS

1½ cups all-purpose flour

¾ cup Dutch processed cocoa, such as Droste®

1 teaspoon baking soda

½ teaspoon fine sea salt

¾ cup canola oil

½ cup sugar

½ cup firmly packed light brown sugar

1 large egg, lightly beaten

½ cup white chocolate or parve white chocolate chips; can use regular chocolate chips instead

½ cup chopped walnuts, optional

A combo of brownies and biscotti, these cookies are so quick to whip together you'll find you'll make them over and over.

1. Preheat oven to 350°F.

2. Line a large cookie sheet with parchment paper. Set aside.

3. In a medium bowl, mix the flour, cocoa, baking soda, and salt. Set aside.

4. In a large mixing bowl, using a sturdy wooden spoon, mix the oil, sugar, and brown sugar until smooth. Mix in the egg.

5. Stir in half the cocoa mixture and mix until a smooth dough forms. Stir in the rest of the cocoa mixture. Knead the dough with both hands for 1 minute. Mix in the chocolate chips and walnuts, if using. Use your hands to knead them into the dough.

6. Transfer half the dough to the prepared sheet. Using the parchment paper to assist, form the dough into a long log, 3–4 inches wide. Repeat with remaining dough. Leave 2–3 inches of space between the logs to allow for spreading.

7. Bake for 25 minutes.

8. Remove from oven and cool for 10 minutes. Slide the parchment paper off the cookie sheet. This will give you room to cut the logs into sticks when they have cooled. Using a serrated knife, cut cooled logs into ¾-inch slices. Transfer to serving plate.

No-Bake Dulce de Leche Cheesecake

DAIRY ■ YIELDS 8 SERVINGS

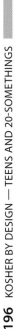

1 cup chilled heavy whipping cream

¼ cup sugar

⅓ cup water

1¾ teaspoons unflavored gelatin (I like Kolatin®)

1 (8-ounce) bar cream cheese, very soft, not whipped

½ cup dulce de leche or butterscotch-caramel topping, warmed for 30 seconds in microwave

1 (9-inch) ready-to-serve graham cracker crust

additional dulce de leche for drizzling

Dulce de leche is a thick, rich caramel sauce that is found near the ice cream toppings. Butterscotch-caramel ice cream topping is a stand-in if you can't find real dulce de leche. Either way, you will love this dreamy dessert and you won't believe how easy this no-bake cheesecake is. Unflavored gelatin is the magic ingredient. I use the Kolatin® brand of gelatin for the best hold.

1. In the bowl of a stand mixer, beat the whipped cream on medium just until stiff peaks form. Transfer to another bowl. Set aside.

2. In a small saucepan, mix the sugar into the water; sprinkle the gelatin over the water. Let stand until softened and the gelatin is translucent.

3. Over medium low heat, slowly warm the gelatin mix until the sugar and gelatin dissolve, about 2–4 minutes. Scrape sides and stir often with a rubber scraper. Set aside to cool slightly.

4. Using the mixer, in a medium bowl, beat the cream cheese and dulce de leche until it is thoroughly combined.

5. Slowly beat in the gelatin mix until smooth. Add the whipped cream and beat until smooth and soft peaks form.

6. Dollop into the prepared crust and use an offset spatula to smooth the top. Refrigerate at least 3 hours.

7. Before serving, warm the desired amount of dulce de leche for 30 seconds in the microwave. Drizzle the top of the cheesecake with the warmed dulce de leche.

Coconut Angel Food Cake

PARVE ■ YIELDS 12 SERVINGS

12 large egg whites, at room temperature (see step 3 in recipe for method)

1¼ teaspoons cream of tartar

½ teaspoon fine sea salt

1 teaspoon coconut extract

½ teaspoon pure vanilla extract

1½ cups superfine sugar

1 cup cake flour (not self-rising), sifted

2 cups confectioner's sugar

¼ cup plus 1 tablespoon canned coconut milk (NOT cream of coconut)

shredded sweetened flaked coconut

Just a crash course on some of the ingredients in this recipe: Cake flour is a special kind of flour that has less protein than all-purpose flour. It is not as heavy, so it will give a very tender and light result when needed, such as in a light and airy cake like Angel Food. Self-rising cake flour, which we do not want in this recipe, has baking powder and salt added in. Superfine sugar is regular sugar that has been ground more finely. It dissolves quickly in recipes like this one or in drinks. If you do not have it, just run some regular sugar in your food processor for 20 seconds.

1. Preheat oven to 350°F.

2. Cover the base of a 10-inch tube pan with parchment circles. If you can't find the rounds with a pre-cut hole for angel food pans, cut your own out of parchment paper. Do NOT grease the pan. Set aside.

3. Holding a hand with palm facing up over the bowl of an electric mixer, crack an egg, letting the whites slip through your fingers into the bowl and setting the yolk aside for another use. Repeat with all the eggs. Make sure there are no yellow specks in the whites or they won't whip up properly.

4. In the bowl of an electric mixer fitted with whisk attachment, beat the egg whites on medium until foamy. Beat in cream of tartar, salt, and coconut and vanilla extracts. Raise speed to medium-high and beat to soft peaks. Reduce speed to low and beat in the superfine sugar, a large spoonful at a time. Beat until stiff but moist-looking peaks form.

5. Using a spatula, carefully fold the flour, ¼ cup at a time, into the egg whites, taking care not to deflate the egg whites.

6. Spoon the mixture into the ungreased lined tube pan. Cut through the batter with a knife to break any air pockets. Bake for 35–40 minutes, until top is spongy to the touch and toothpick inserted in center comes out clean.

7. Cool the cake in the pan by hanging it upside down on a wine bottle or, if your pan has legs, upside down on a cooling rack for at least an hour before removing from the pan. Slide a narrow spatula around the sides of the pan to separate the cake from the sides. Remove from pan and cool completely on a cake plate.

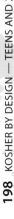

8. In a small bowl, whisk the confectioner's sugar with the coconut milk until smooth and the consistency of glue. Pour the glaze over the top of the cake, using a small spatula to help it run over the sides. Immediately press flaked coconut into the glaze, covering the whole cake. Slice with serrated knife.

Easy Fudge

DAIRY ■ YIELDS 12-16 SERVINGS

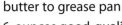

butter to grease pan

16 ounces good-quality milk chocolate bar, such as Ghiradelli®

1 (14-ounce) can sweetened condensed milk

4 tablespoons unsalted butter, cut into chunks

If all you have in the house are chocolate chips, you can substitute in 3 cups of good-quality chips for the 16 ounces of chocolate bars. You can also melt 1 cup of peanut butter chips in the microwave and, once the fudge is poured into the pan, use a knife to swirl in the melted peanut butter chips for a marbled effect. You can also set nuts like chopped cashews, walnuts, or almonds into the fudge, as well as mini marshmallows, shredded coconut, or butterscotch chips.

1. Butter a 9-by-9-inch square Pyrex or baking pan. Trim a piece of parchment paper to line the bottom and sides of the pan, leaving extra parchment to overhang on all sides. This will help with unmolding the fudge when it is done. Set aside.

2. Create a double boiler by filling a small-medium pot with a few inches of water. Set a glass or metal mixing bowl onto the pot so that it is snug and won't move around. The bottom of the mixing bowl should not touch the water in the pot. You also want to make sure that no water gets into the chocolate mixture or it won't melt smoothly. Turn the heat to medium and allow the water to simmer.

3. Meanwhile, break the chocolate bars as you place them into the bowl. Add the sweetened condensed milk and butter.

4. As the gentle heat starts to melt the ingredients, stir and make sure to scrape down the sides of the bowl.

5. Once the chocolate mixture is melted, creamy, and slightly thick, remove bowl from pot. Carefully wipe hot water droplets from the bottom of the bowl. Use your spatula to scrape the mixture into the prepared pan.

6. Cool for a few minutes and then place into the refrigerator to cool completely, about 2 hours, until solid and fudge-like.

7. Using the parchment paper, lift the fudge out of the pan and place onto a cutting board. Cut into squares.

8. Refrigerate if not eating right away.

Blondies

DAIRY OR PARVE ■ **YIELDS 9 SERVINGS**

1 cup all-purpose flour

1 teaspoon baking powder

¼ teaspoon fine sea salt

½ cup (1 stick) unsalted butter or margarine

1 cup firmly packed light brown sugar

1 large egg

1 teaspoon pure vanilla extract

¾ cup semisweet chocolate chips

These blondies are a blank canvas for mix-ins. Try ¾ cup walnuts, pecans, Heath bits®, or coconut. Light brown sugar makes a difference, so don't use dark. This is a low-maintenance recipe: it needs no stand mixer; the blondies freeze well, and the recipe doubles easily into a 9-by-13-inch pan. Just increase the baking time by 15-20 minutes. If you don't like the chocolate chips to look melty, but rather retain their shape, store them in the refrigerator and use them cold.

1. Preheat oven to 350°F.

2. Line a 9-by-9-inch baking pan with foil or parchment paper. Lightly grease if using foil. Set aside.

3. In a medium bowl, whisk the flour, baking powder, and sea salt. Set aside.

4. Place the butter or margarine into a large pot over low heat. Gently melt it. Remove from heat and, using a wooden spoon, mix in the light brown sugar and stir until mixed well and the sugar is melted. Cool for 5 minutes. Quickly whisk in the egg. Add the vanilla and whisk again. With the wooden spoon, slowly add the flour mixture, stirring to incorporate. Mix in the chocolate chips or any other add-in.

5. Scrape the batter into the prepared pan, using a small spatula to smooth it evenly into the corners. Level the top.

6. Bake for 25–30 minutes.

7. Cool completely before cutting into bars. Don't overbake or the blondies will loose their signature chewiness.

White Graham Clusters

DAIRY ■ YIELDS 12-14 SERVINGS

2 (4-ounce) good-quality white chocolate bars, such as Ghiradelli®

2 cups Golden Grahams® cereal

2 cups salted pretzel sticks, broken to fit into the measuring cup

These are addictive. Feel free to add chopped cashew nuts or almonds to the mix as well.

1. Line a cookie sheet or jelly roll pan with parchment paper. Set aside.

2. Break the white chocolate into pieces and place into a large microwave-safe bowl. Microwave at 50% power for 40 seconds at a time, stirring each time to hasten the melting, until the chocolate is smooth, melted, and creamy.

3. Mix in the cereal and pretzels, coating well with the white chocolate.

4. Spread onto the prepared sheet; you will fill only half of a standard cookie sheet.

5. Cool and harden at room temperature for 3–4 hours, or more quickly in the refrigerator. Break into clusters.

6. Serve in paper muffin cups.

Yum!

Red Velvet Cupcakes

DAIRY ■ YIELDS 24 CUPCAKES

CUPCAKES:

2½ cups all-purpose flour

½ cup Dutch processed cocoa (I like Droste®)

½ teaspoon fine sea salt

1 cup (2 sticks) butter, softened for 15 minutes at room temperature

2 cups sugar

4 large eggs

1 cup reduced-fat sour cream, but not fat-free

¾ cup low-fat milk

1 teaspoon pure vanilla extract

1 (1-ounce) bottle red food coloring

1 teaspoon white vinegar

1 teaspoon baking soda

FROSTING:

1 (8-ounce) block cream cheese, softened for 15 minutes at room temperature

½ cup (1 stick) butter, softened for 15 minutes at room temperature

2 cups confectioner's sugar

1 teaspoon pure vanilla extract

If you are lucky, you have neighbors whose kids feel like extended family. Aviva and Nina Kahn are those kids to me. They recently went on a family road trip to visit with relatives in Atlanta. While they were there, they sampled Red Velvet Cupcakes, a favorite down South. The next week, they came knocking on my door with red-stained hands to deliver a batch of the cupcakes for me to sample, along with their 3 pages of handwritten recipe with notes. Just one more reason why I love those girls.

Some of their tips: Wear disposable gloves to avoid the red-stained-hand issue and wear an apron. Substitute Tofutti cream cheese and sour cream, margarine, and soy milk for a parve version. The parve frosting will be thin. Add confectioner's sugar, ¼ cup at a time until it becomes creamy. If making in advance, refrigerate the frosting and frost before using; store the cupcakes in an airtight container. Store in refrigerator if not eating right away.

1. Preheat oven to 350°F. Line 2 cupcake tins (12 cups each) with paper liners.

2. In a medium bowl, whisk the flour, cocoa, and salt. Set aside.

3. In the bowl of a stand mixer, at medium speed, beat the butter until light and fluffy, about 2 minutes. Add the sugar and beat for 3 minutes more until very light and fluffy.

4. Add the eggs, one at a time, mixing after each one. Add the sour cream, milk, vanilla, and food coloring.

5. Pour the vinegar into a ¼-cup measuring cup. Add the baking soda; stir. It will bubble and fizz. Add it to the batter and mix for just a few seconds; do not over-mix once the baking soda is added. At low speed, add the flour mixture. Scrape down the sides with a silicone spatula.

6. Spoon into the prepared pans, filling each liner two-thirds full.

7. Bake for 20–22 minutes, until a toothpick inserted in the center of a cupcake comes out clean. Remove from oven. Transfer cupcakes to a rack to cool completely.

8. Once the cupcakes are cool, prepare the frosting: In the bowl of a stand mixer, beat the cream cheese, butter, confectioner's sugar, and vanilla until light and fluffy, about 5 minutes. Spread on completely cooled cupcakes.

Snowball Cookies

½ cup (1 stick) butter or margarine, softened at room temperature for 20 minutes

⅓ cup sugar

1 cup all-purpose flour

1 teaspoon pure vanilla extract

confectioner's sugar

Could there be a more perfect time to have worked on this recipe than a 2-day "snow-day" off from school? Luckily I had plenty of hungry happy kids on hand to give opinions, and they loved this light-as-snow cookie. Warning: Powdered sugar will be everywhere!

This recipe can also be made in a food processor fitted with the metal "S" blade. Pulse the butter and sugar until creamy, then add the flour and vanilla, pulsing until combined.

1. Preheat oven to 325°F. Line a cookie sheet with parchment paper. Set aside.

2. In the small bowl of a stand mixer, at medium speed, beat the butter or margarine and sugar until light and creamy.

3. Add the flour and vanilla. Mix until well blended, scraping the sides as necessary. The dough may look a little crumbly.

4. Pinch and roll into 1-inch balls and place on prepared sheet.

5. Bake for 18 minutes until slightly golden. Allow to cool for 5 minutes.

6. Pour confectioner's sugar into a ziplock bag or a bowl. Add the cookies, a few at a time, and coat completely in the powdered sugar. You may toss them in the sugar again after they have cooled completely.

Cappuccino Mousse

DAIRY OR PARVE ■ YIELDS 4-6 SERVINGS

CAPPUCCINO MOUSSE:

9 ounces good-quality milk or semisweet chocolate (I like Ghiradelli®)

4 teaspoons instant espresso powder or instant coffee

¼ cup cold water

1½ cups heavy cream or nondairy whipped topping (I like Richwhip®)

CHOCOLATE-DIPPED SPOON GARNISH:

plastic spoons

1 (4-ounce) good-quality semisweet chocolate or white chocolate bar (I like Ghiradelli®), chopped

whipped cream, optional for garnish

One of my tasters said, "The dairy version of this recipe tastes like Starbucks on steroids!" It is a creamy dream. To make the parve version, adjust by using only 6 ounces of good-quality semisweet chocolate and whip 3 tablespoons of sugar into the nondairy whipping cream to keep the sweetness at the correct level.

1. On a cutting board, finely chop the chocolate. Transfer the chopped chocolate and any shavings into a microwave-safe bowl.

2. In a small bowl, dissolve the espresso or coffee in the water. Add it to the chocolate.

3. With the microwave set to 70% power, melt the chocolate in 30-second intervals, stirring between each round to hasten the melting. Stir until completely smooth and melted.

4. In the bowl of a stand mixer fitted with the whisk attachment, whip the heavy cream until stiff peaks form. Do not overbeat. Using a silicone spatula, gently fold the chocolate into the whipped cream until it is an even coffee color. Immediately spoon into glass or ceramic mugs, teacups, or other serving bowl. The mousse will set quickly, so work rapidly.

5. Prepare the chocolate-dipped spoon garnish: Place the chopped chocolate into a small microwave-safe bowl. Microwave at 70% power for 30 seconds at a time, stirring at each interval to hasten the melting, until smooth and melted. Repeat in 30-second intervals until chocolate is smooth and fully melted. Dip plastic spoons into the chocolate to coat the bowl of each spoon. Lay spoons on parchment paper to set. To speed the process, you can place the spoons into the refrigerator to set for 5 minutes. Serve with the cappuccino mousse. Top the mousse with whipped cream if desired.

Lemon Crumb Cake

DAIRY OR PARVE ■ YIELDS 15 SERVINGS

CRUMB TOPPING:

1 cup sugar

zest of 1 lemon

½ cup (1 stick) butter or margarine, melted

1 tablespoon fresh lemon juice (about the juice of ½ lemon)

1¼ cups all-purpose flour

LEMON CAKE:

nonstick spray with flour

3 cups all-purpose flour

1½ cups sugar

1 tablespoon baking powder

1 teaspoon fine sea salt

2 large eggs

2 tablespoons fresh lemon juice (about the juice of 1 lemon)

1 cup milk or soy milk

1 cup (2 sticks) butter or margarine, melted

A delicious burst of moist lemon flavor. Perfect with a cup of tea or for a sweet treat in your lunch bag. In the summertime when gorgeous blueberries abound, feel free to stir a handful into the batter.

1. Prepare the crumb topping: In a medium bowl combine the cup of sugar with the lemon zest. Rub the sugar mixture between your palms to distribute the zest. Add the butter or margarine, lemon juice, and flour. Using a wooden spoon, stir until the mixture is crumbly. Set aside.

2. Set the rack into the center of the oven. Preheat oven to 350°F. Spray a 9-by-13-inch baking pan with nonstick spray. If you don't have the spray with flour, spray with regular nonstick spray, drizzle 1 tablespoon flour over the pan, and then shake to distribute it.

3. In a medium bowl, whisk the flour, sugar, baking powder, and salt. Set aside.

4. In the bowl of a stand mixer at medium speed, beat the eggs, lemon juice, milk or soy milk, and melted butter or margarine.

5. Add the flour mixture and beat just until a smooth batter forms.

6. Pour the batter into the prepared pan, using a spatula to spread it evenly.

7. Sprinkle the crumb topping over the top of the cake. Bake, uncovered, for 40–45 minutes, or until a toothpick inserted in the center of the cake comes out clean.

8. Allow to cool completely before serving.

Molten Deep-Dish Chocolate Chip Cookies

DAIRY OR PARVE ■ YIELDS 10-12 SERVINGS DEPENDING ON SIZE

2¼ cups all-purpose flour

1 teaspoon baking soda

1 teaspoon fine sea salt

1 cup (2 sticks) butter or margarine, at room temperature for 15 minutes

¾ cup sugar

¾ cup light brown sugar

1 teaspoon pure vanilla extract

2 large eggs

1 (12-ounce) bag best-quality chocolate chips (2 cups)

high heat or professional cooking spray

1 (4-ounce) good-quality semisweet chocolate bar (I like Schmerling Noblesse® for parve), broken into pieces on the score marks

These are awesome!! I based this recipe on my girlfriend Yael Eisenberg's famous cookies. I make this version in 4-ounce disposable aluminum muffin tins. The cookies come out of them very easily. However, each time I go to buy them, the sizes are different from store-to-store. This means they will vary in volume, but you really can't ruin this dish — just watch baking times. Smaller tins will bake faster and you want these a bit underdone. Larger tins can be used for a 2-person portion; just use more dough and bake slightly longer. If you prepare the molten cookies in 4-inch ceramic ramekins, the cookies will be harder to remove but just as yummy, so just serve right in the ramekin. You can even top them off with some ice cream. Just warn your friends that the ramekin will be warm to the touch.

You can make the dough in advance and keep in the fridge so that you can enjoy this treat at a moment's notice! If serving for Friday night, bake right before Shabbos and keep warm on a blech or warming tray.

1. Preheat oven to 350°F.

2. In a medium bowl, whisk the flour, baking soda, and salt. Set aside.

3. In the bowl of a stand mixer, at medium-low speed, mix the butter or margarine with the sugar and brown sugar. Raise the speed to medium-high and mix until creamy, light, and fluffy. Turn the speed down a little. Add the vanilla and eggs. Mix to incorporate.

4. Add half the flour mixture. Mix. Add the remaining flour mixture and mix until just combined. Mix in the chocolate chips.

5. Spray the aluminum tins with nonstick cooking spray.

6. Fill each muffin cup or ramekin a quarter of the way with a large, ping-pong-ball-size ball of cookie dough. Flatten slightly to cover the bottom. Stack 2 chocolate squares in the center. Cover with a second walnut-sized ball of cookie dough, flattening it to completely cover the chocolate.

7. Place onto a cookie sheet and bake until tops are golden brown. Do not overbake or the end result will be doughy, not gooey. The baking time will vary from 20–25 minutes depending on the size of the tin or ramekin and the amount of dough you needed to fill it. You are looking for the tops to be golden and not wet-looking.

8. If using aluminum tins, turn each cookie out onto a plate. Serve warm.

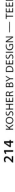

The way to go!

Gatherings

So fun!

Get-together

Celebrate!

Let's PARTY
PLAY BALL

Wondering how to gather a group of guys together? Need time to kick back with friends while competing just a bit? Well, look no further than America's Favorite Pastime, and **play ball!** Baseball can be used in many ways to host a fun party.

Take your party to the park and play a game for charity, watch a big game as a group, celebrate the end of leagues, or get together to burn off some excess summer energy. Whatever the reason, a baseball theme is sure to be a home run!

We decided to bring a bit of the ballpark into our home. Here are some ideas to create your own baseball bash.

Hang old **pennants** or uniforms around the party room. Set up a smaller table off to the side as a concession stand. Load it with popcorn, peanuts, hot pretzels, cotton candy — all the ballpark favorites.

Cover a table with fake grass or Astroturf (available at home improvement stores). Gather your *baseball paraphernalia* — mini helmets, baseball cards, hats, bats, balls, cleats, bases, even your old Little League trophies … anything baseball related. Arrange them down the center of a table. The more "stuff" you use, the better the table will look. Use this as the buffet on which to serve the food. Put out plates; wood or recycled bamboo would look great here. Wrap the silverware in mini-pennants that you can buy or print off the internet. Hang mini helmets from the tops of water bottles or soda cans. Autograph a ball or bat with your team name or logo.

Have the words to "Take Me Out to the Ballgame" handy for a 7th inning stretch sing-along.

Serve appropriate food like Big Dogs (see page 18) or Meatball Subs (see page 106). Pour something thirst-quenching, like Raspberry Iced Tea (see page 36).

Before your friends leave, don't forget to pose with them for a team picture.

Remember …
if you host it,
they will come!

Let's PARTY
BACKYARD BASH

So you've spent all that time mowing it, seeding it, and weeding it — let's turn that backyard botanical garden of yours into a getaway experience for your guests with an old-fashioned backyard bash!

Set up a clothesline or volleyball net. Using clothespins, clip *summer-themed* items to it, including hula hoops, flipflops, sunglasses, pinwheels, flyswatters, and brightly colored toys. Using fabric paints, write the menu on a big, clean white T-shirt and clip it onto the net as well.

Arrange large pillows or mats under the shade of a market umbrella where your friends can *cool off, chill out, lounge around*, and be protected from the sun. Hang flyswatters and paper lanterns from the umbrella, for a splash of color and a whimsical feel.

Artfully arrange some citronella candles to keep the bugs at bay. Set out buckets of sunscreen, bug spray, misters — and don't forget disposable digital cameras so your friends can capture the fun for you. Make sure to have plenty of ice and cold drinks on hand. Something *refreshing* like Pink-Berry Lemonade (see page 46) can be your featured

drink. Scatter around assorted balls, badminton rackets, and paddle balls so your friends can get the party started.

If any of your friends play an instrument like the guitar or harmonica, encourage them to bring it along and help entertain.

Serve dinner when you see the first twinkling lights in the sky. A large galvanized bucket within reach of the garden hose makes for a gorgeous washing station. Hang *netillat yadaim* cups from the side and float a few beautiful blooms in the cups and bucket. Dinner can be served on trays for easy transfer to the backyard. For a playful idea, serve dinner

or dessert in colorful *Frisbees!* Make sure that the food you serve tastes good at room temperature so you are not tied to your oven. This allows you to be with your guests once the food is set out on the buffet.

Toss out a glow-in-the-dark volleyball and keep the party going even after the sun goes down.

*H*ere's a creative and inexpensive way to transform friends from bored to on board! Host your own energetic game night! But even a casual night of fun requires a game plan. Based on the sophistication and age range of your guests, you can choose from a variety of games to set a mood or establish a theme.

For a *retro feel*, bring out the games that are older than your parents — like Scrabble, Sorry, Pictionary, Risk, Monopoly, Trivial Pursuit — and for the really daring — Candy Land! Into history, are you? Some of the oldest games in the world are chess, backgammon, checkers, Chinese checkers, and the Royal Game of Ur (see Wikipedia!). There are board games today to fit so many theme possibilities. You could even have a *BYOBG* (bring your own board game) party!

Here's how to duplicate a board game night that was a huge success at my house:

Break out all the games in your house. Spread a Twister board out on the floor; this will serve the

dual purpose of setting the atmosphere and catching any crumbs from the food portion of the party. Arrange a bunch of the boxed games that you will not likely be playing into a table. If you need stability, build it around a milk crate or sturdy box. Open a large game board to use as your tabletop. The *childhood game* Ants in Your Pants makes the perfect container to hold an arrangement of flowers. Just stick a piece of Styrofoam or floral oasis into the "pants" and poke the flowers into it. For a simpler centerpiece, slide a single stemmed flower or two into the slightly unzipped bag of Bananagrams.

Avoid one- and two-player games, since this is supposed to be a party. You might have a couple of single- or double-player games in reserve in a basket, in case your group plays elimination games, so those who are "out" can stay involved until the next round of games.

Of course, when friends gather, there must be food! *Plan a menu* that works with this kind of party. If the action of the games is to continue, you will need to serve food that can be eaten while playing, won't be too sticky or messy, and won't take up too much room at the table. The menu should consist of transportable foods if

you will be holding your party in a den, a game room, or basement.

I printed my menu as a take-off on the classic Monopoly card and served the foods in *interesting portable containers*. The Cheddar Cauliflower Soup (see page 64) was ladled into Ball jars that had lids to avoid splashing as I brought them up the stairs. Banana Pumpkin Cornbread (see page 178) was pre-sliced in the kitchen to avoid crumbs. Even the Fish Tacos (see page 140) were served in a single-serve neat way, propped in drinking glasses for manageable serving.

The dessert, Molten Deep-Dish Chocolate Chip Cookies (see page 214) were served on mini plastic game boards to complete the theme.

So *unplug*, take a breather, reconnect with your friends, and reach back into your childhood for a night that is sure to be memorable.

Let's PARTY
CRAFT NIGHT

It's cold, rainy, dreary, and gets dark early — and you've got a party to plan! Liberate your inner Picasso, *paint the town red*, and throw a crafting party.

A few hours before your guests arrive, cover your table with craft paper or a big white cloth or paper tablecloth. Using brightly colored paints, make handprint designs all over the cloth. Allow it to dry. To continue the *artistic décor*, create a vibrant centerpiece. Set out

a large empty glass vase. Fill it with pom-poms. Top with an inexpensive *artist's palette* and secure with paint brushes. Set out small chalkboards at each place setting to serve as place cards, and add the name of each guest. Position some chalk sticks near each board so your guests can doodle during the party. Pipe cleaners and pom-poms make great napkin rings.

Collect an abundance of art supplies and set them up in empty paint cans on a back table. Markers, scissors, paints, string, glue, assorted papers, brushes, stickers, craft sticks — the more you can add, the better. The variety of color and

materials will allow your guests to really *get creative*.

Of course, creativity inspires the appetite as well as the mind. Here are some food suggestions we enjoyed. Your old kiddy easel is the perfect place to scribble your menu. Keep it simple but make sure to include foods of color and texture like Pizza Soup (see page 62) and Red Velvet Cupcakes (see page 206). For an **amusing food treat**, set out pre-baked waffles or pancakes. Fill squeeze bottles with colorful ice cream toppings and syrups, such as chocolate sauce, strawberry sauce, marshmallow sauce, and caramel topping. Encourage your guests to decorate their food. You can even try it on a spin-art machine. Some models work better than others, but secure your waffle with a dab of peanut butter or marshmallow fluff to keep it from flying off. Get the motor going and the *platform spinning*. Turn the machine off, and with the remaining momentum still turning the waffle, squeeze and decorate away.

This party will be sure to provide you with hours of laughs — and who knows — there may be a *hidden talent* within your group!

Index

O

P

W

Y

Z

Favorite Menu Ideas

My to-go recipes

nutritious snacks

friends favorites

Keep in Stock

Cooking Staples

favorite recipes

Allergy Alert

Also available in the
the Kosher by design®
cookbook series

KOSHER BY DESIGN

- Over 250 luscious recipes
- 120 stunning color photographs
- Holiday menus with complementary wine lists
- Tips on food preparation, table decorations, floral arrangements, and more

ISBN: 978-1-57819-707-1

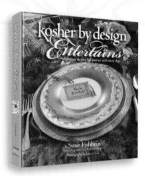

KOSHER BY DESIGN ENTERTAINS

- Over 250 brand-new recipes
- Over 200 stunning color photographs
- Nine different party formats
- Resource Guide: Where to buy unusual kosher ingredients and tableware

ISBN: 978-1-57819-447-6

KOSHER BY DESIGN SHORT ON TIME

- 140 fabulous brand-new recipes
- Large full-color photo featured with every recipe
- Prep time and cooking time
- Innovative ideas for quick and easy table décor

ISBN: 978-1-57819-072-0

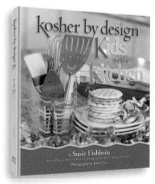

KOSHER BY DESIGN KIDS IN THE KITCHEN

- 80 kid-friendly recipes
- Large full-color photo featured with every recipe
- Equipment lists
- Ingredient lists
- Helpful tips
- Easy-to-follow instructions

ISBN: 978-1-57819-071-3

PASSOVER BY DESIGN

- Over 30 brand-new recipes, many developed with kosher catering star, Moshe David
- Over 100 *Kosher by Design* favorites reformulated and retested for Passover
- Over 140 full-color images throughout, with over 40 brand-new photos
- Table décor and entertaining ideas

ISBN: 978-1-57819-073-7

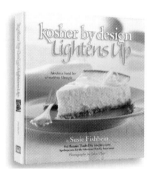

KOSHER BY DESIGN LIGHTENS UP

- Over 145 brand-new recipes
- Large full-color photo featured with every recipe
- Creative new entertaining ideas
- Healthy approaches to oils, sweeteners, and grains
- Tips for smarter shopping and more efficient kitchen gadgets

ISBN: 978-1-57819-117-8